I AM GRATEFUL TO GOD FOR EVERYTHING! AND FOR YOU, HAVE CHOSE THIS COLORING BOOK. C.A, I'M GLAD TO BE MAKING YOU HAVE FUN, THANK YOU VERY MUCH.
LOV U

SARAH ELISA

2024

THIS BOOK BELONGS TO:

_____

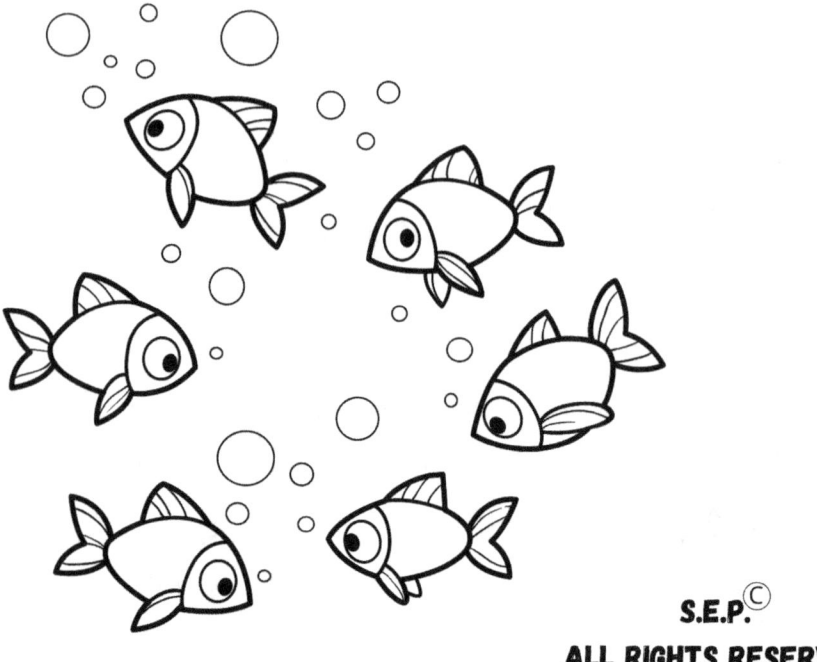

S.E.P.©
ALL RIGHTS RESERVED

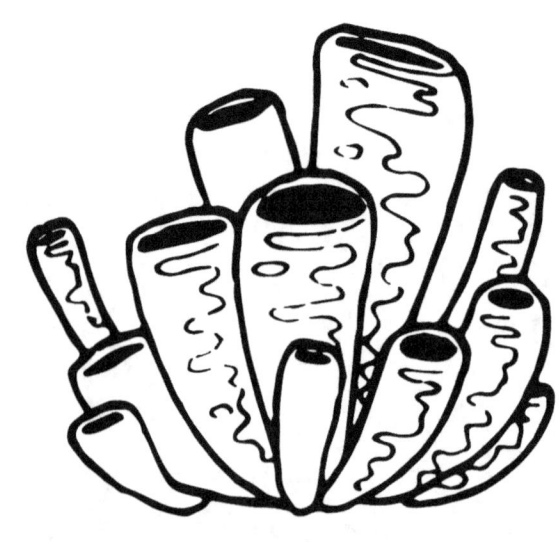

All Rights Reserved ©
2024

No part of this publication may be reproduced, distributed, or transmitted in any form or by any means, including photocopying, recording, or other electronic or mechanical methods, without the prior written permission of the publisher, excerp for brief quotations incorporated in critical reviews and other specific noncommercial uses. Any unauthorized replica of this work is prohibited.

S.E.P.©
SARAH`S ELISA PUBLICATIONS

TEST YOUR COLOR

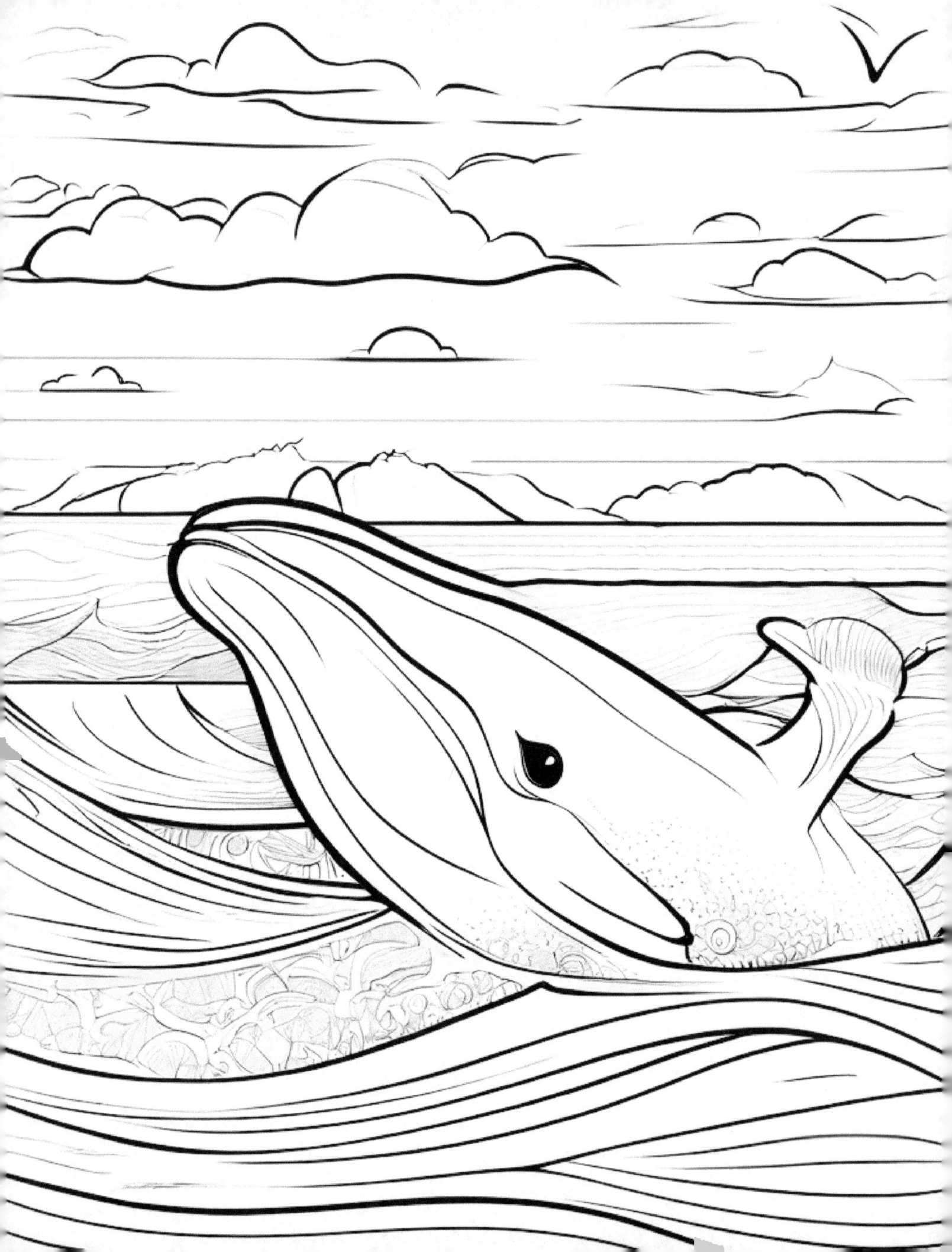

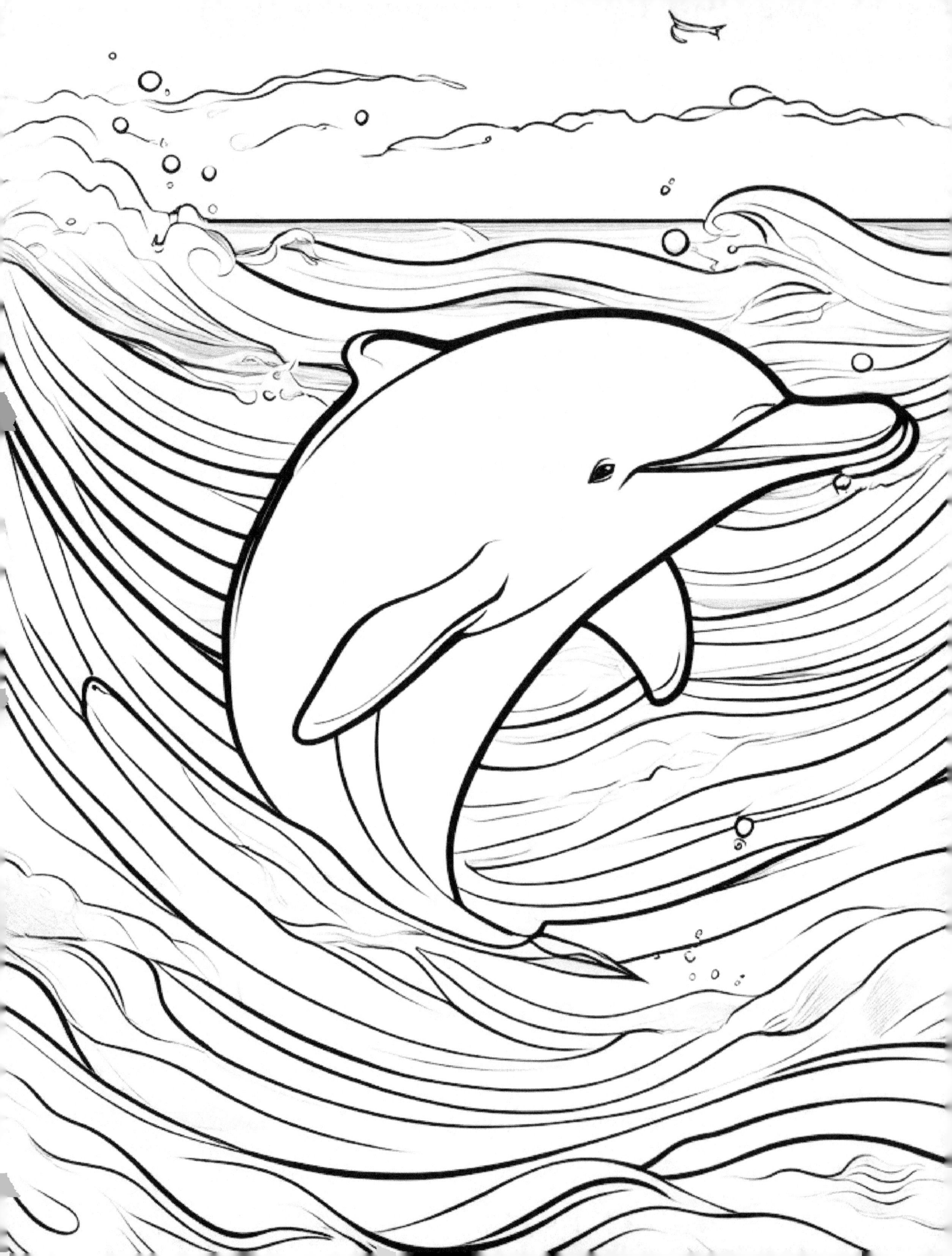

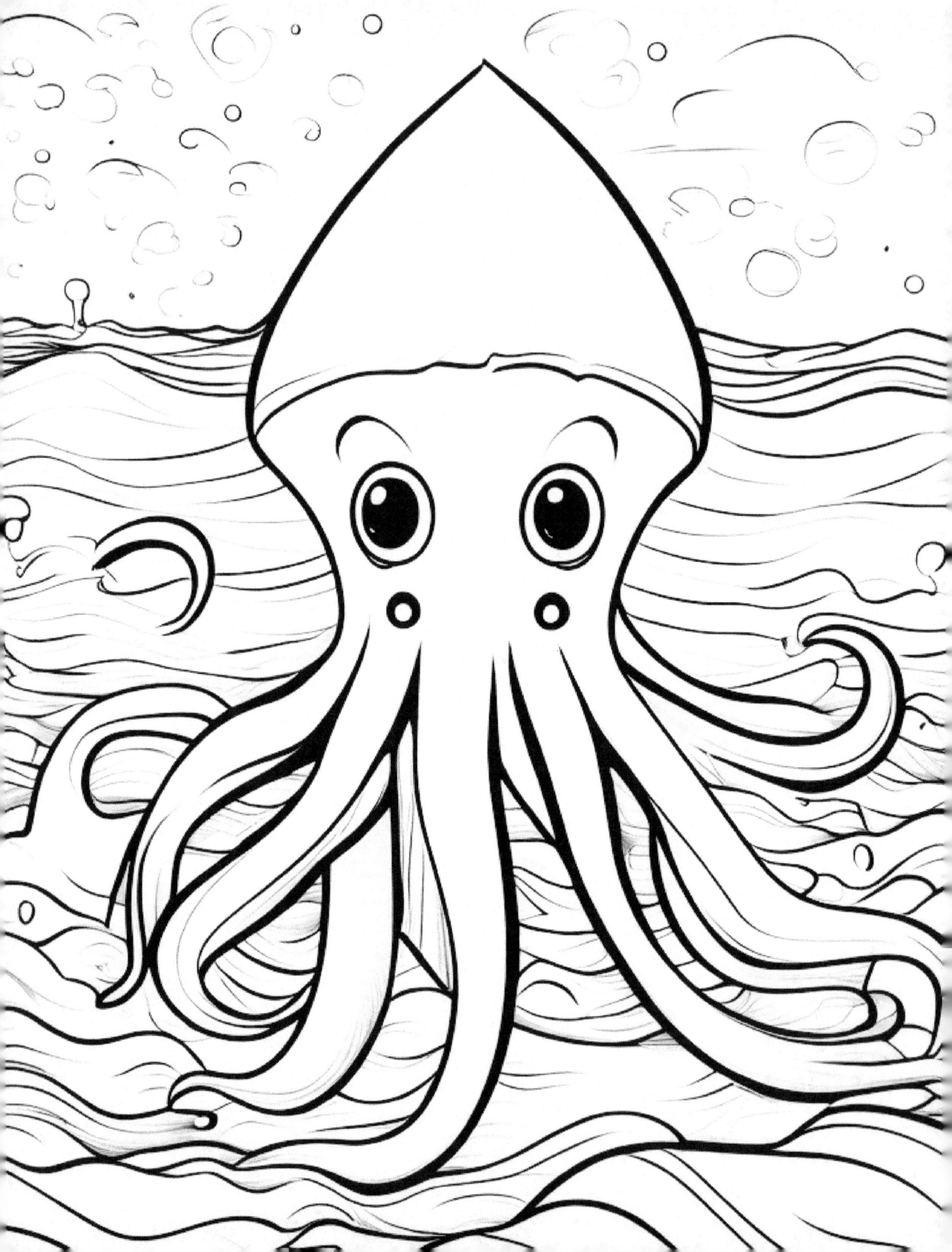

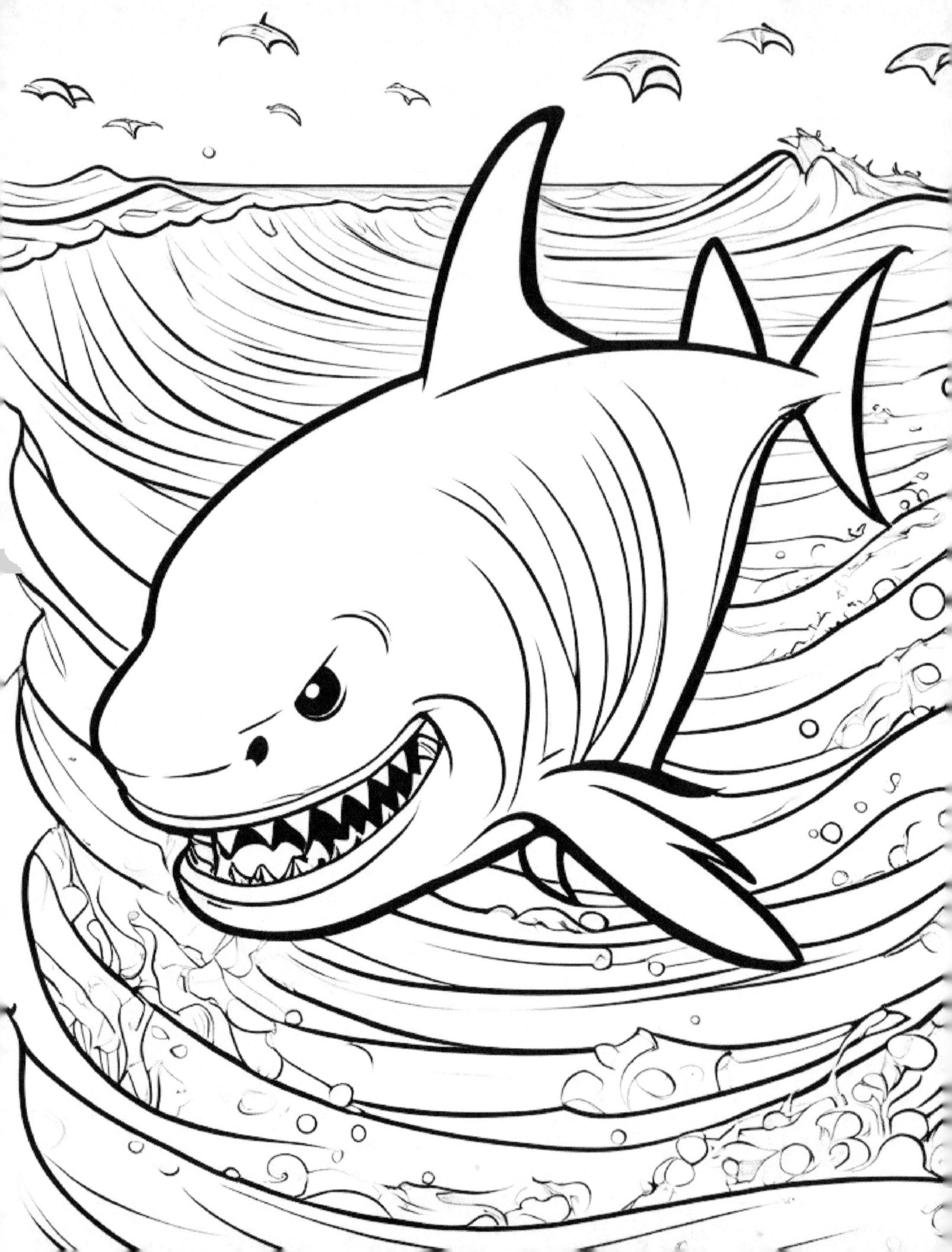

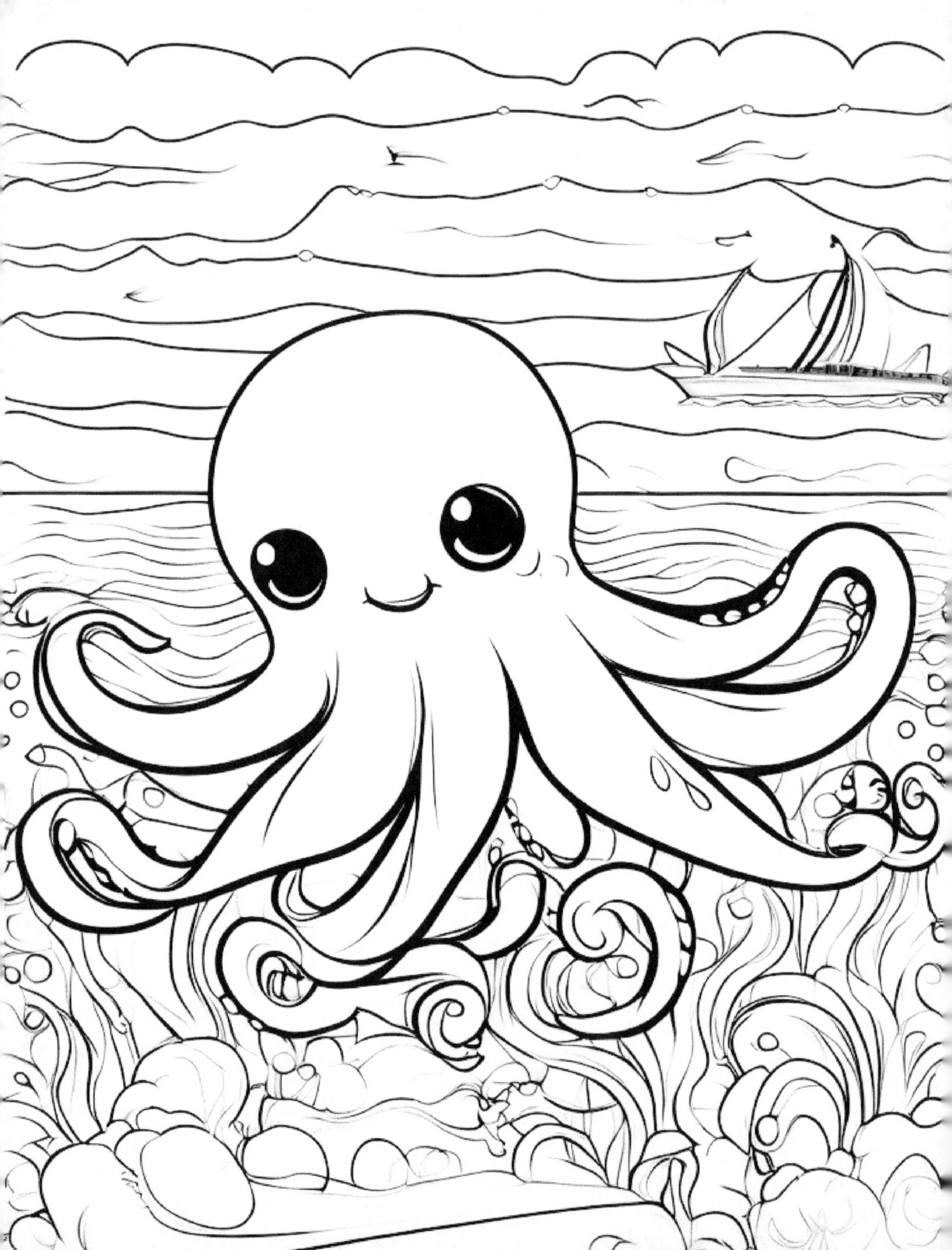

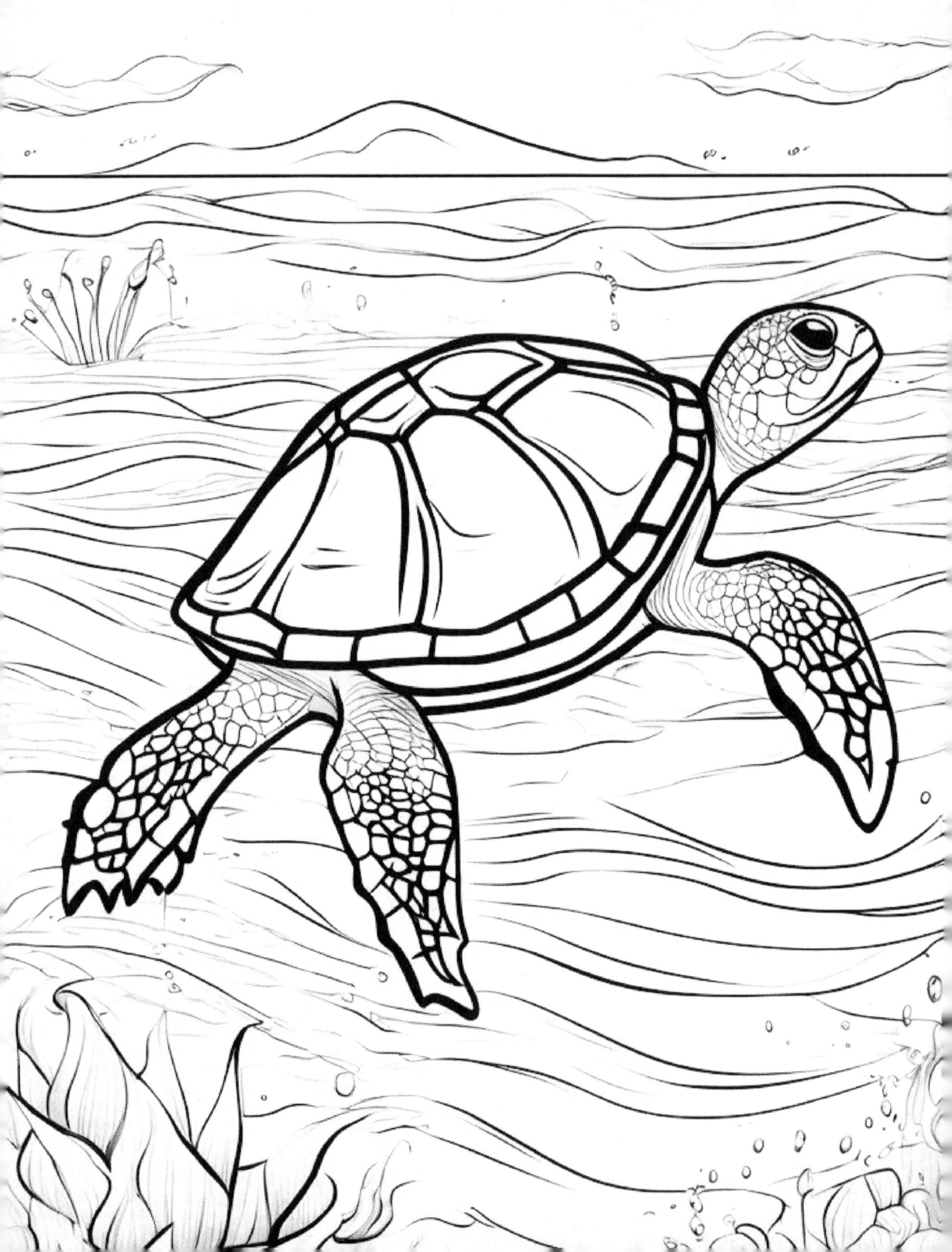

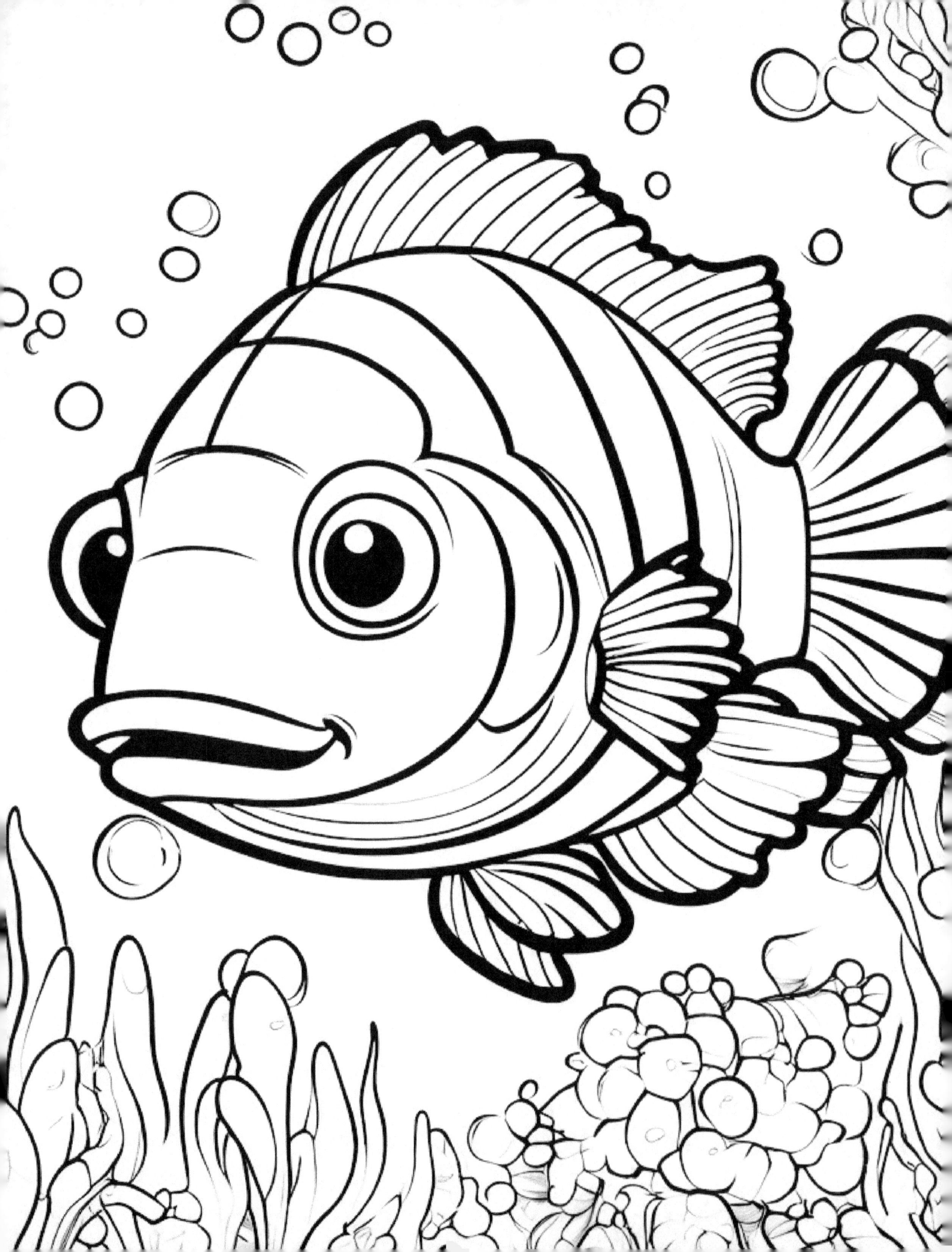

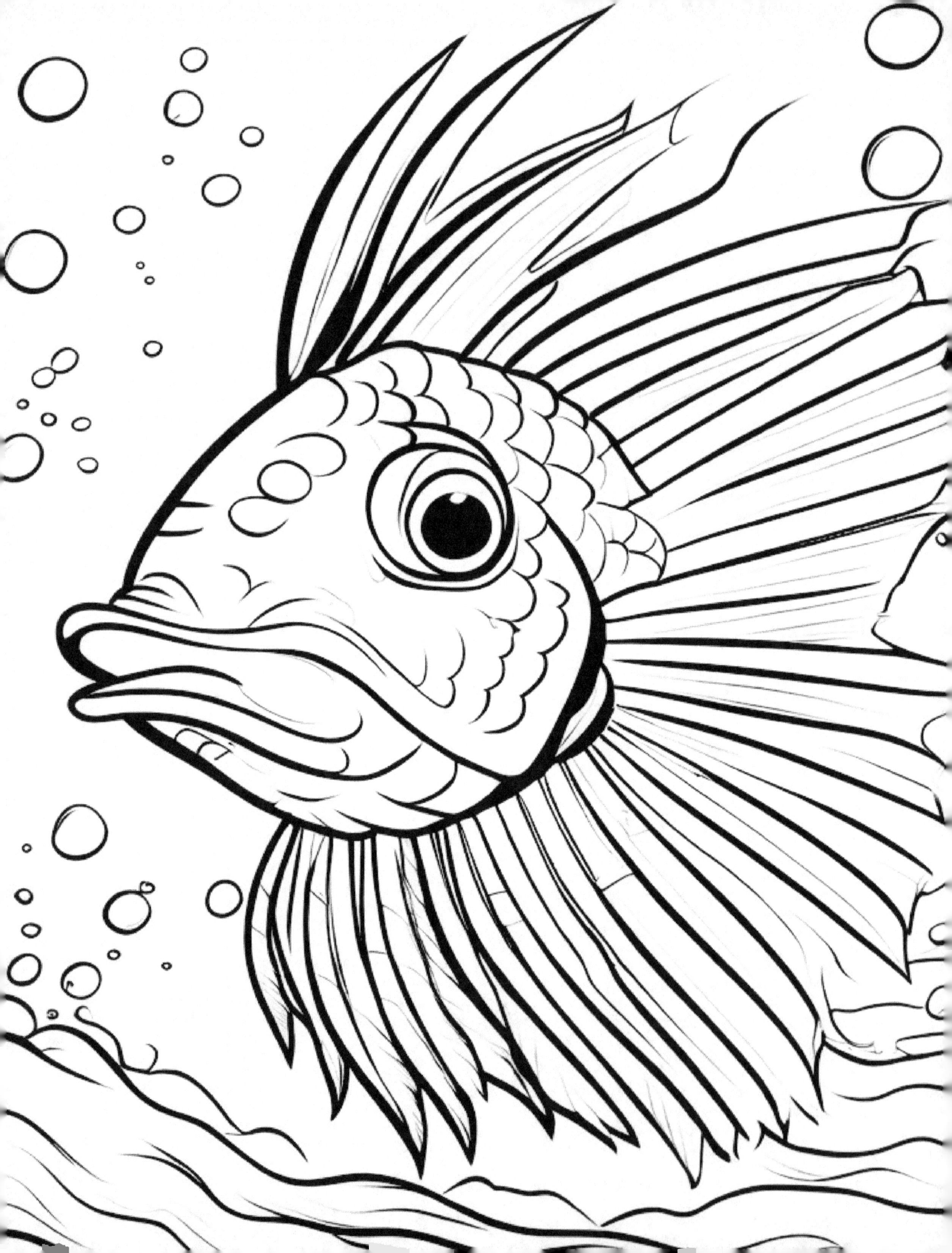

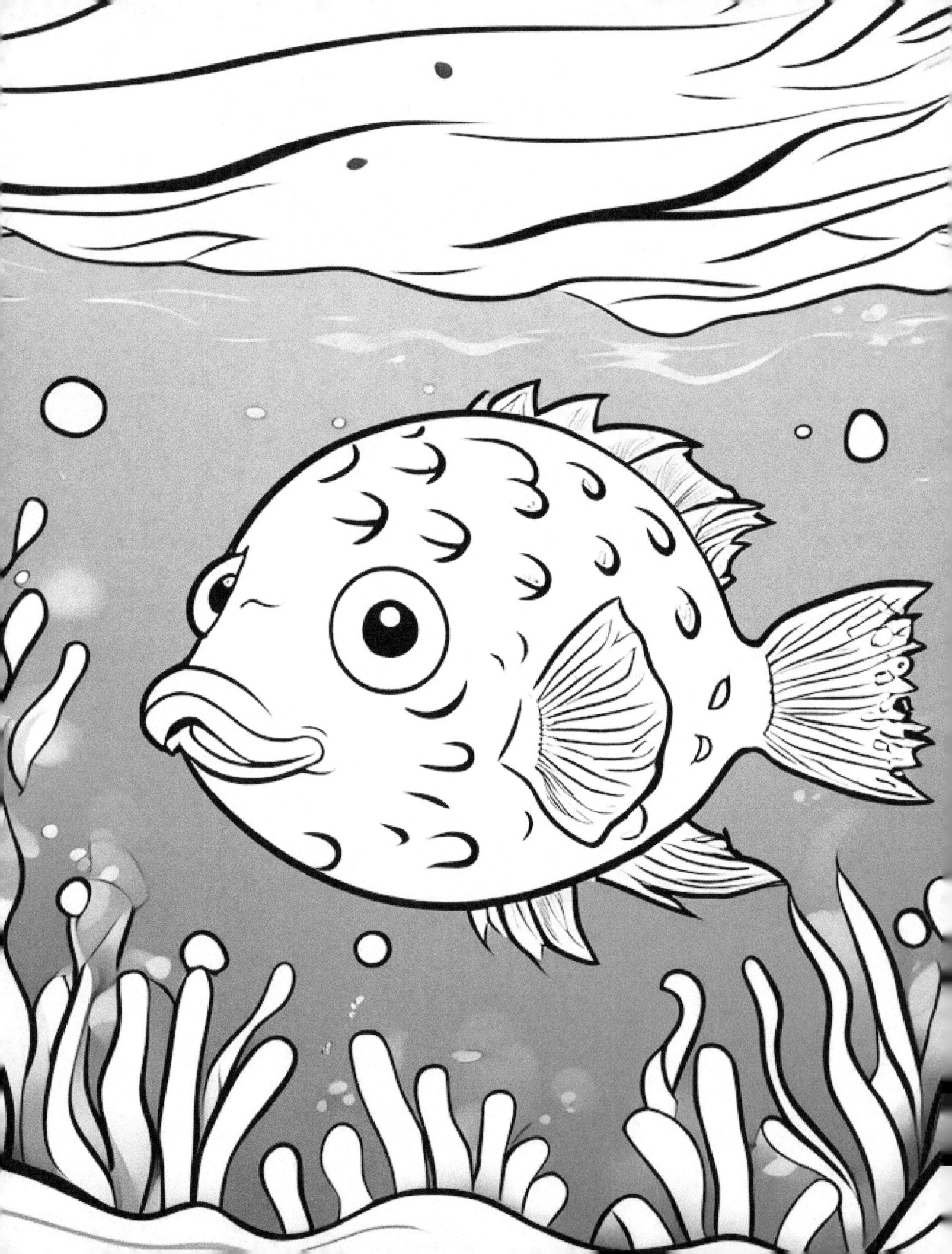

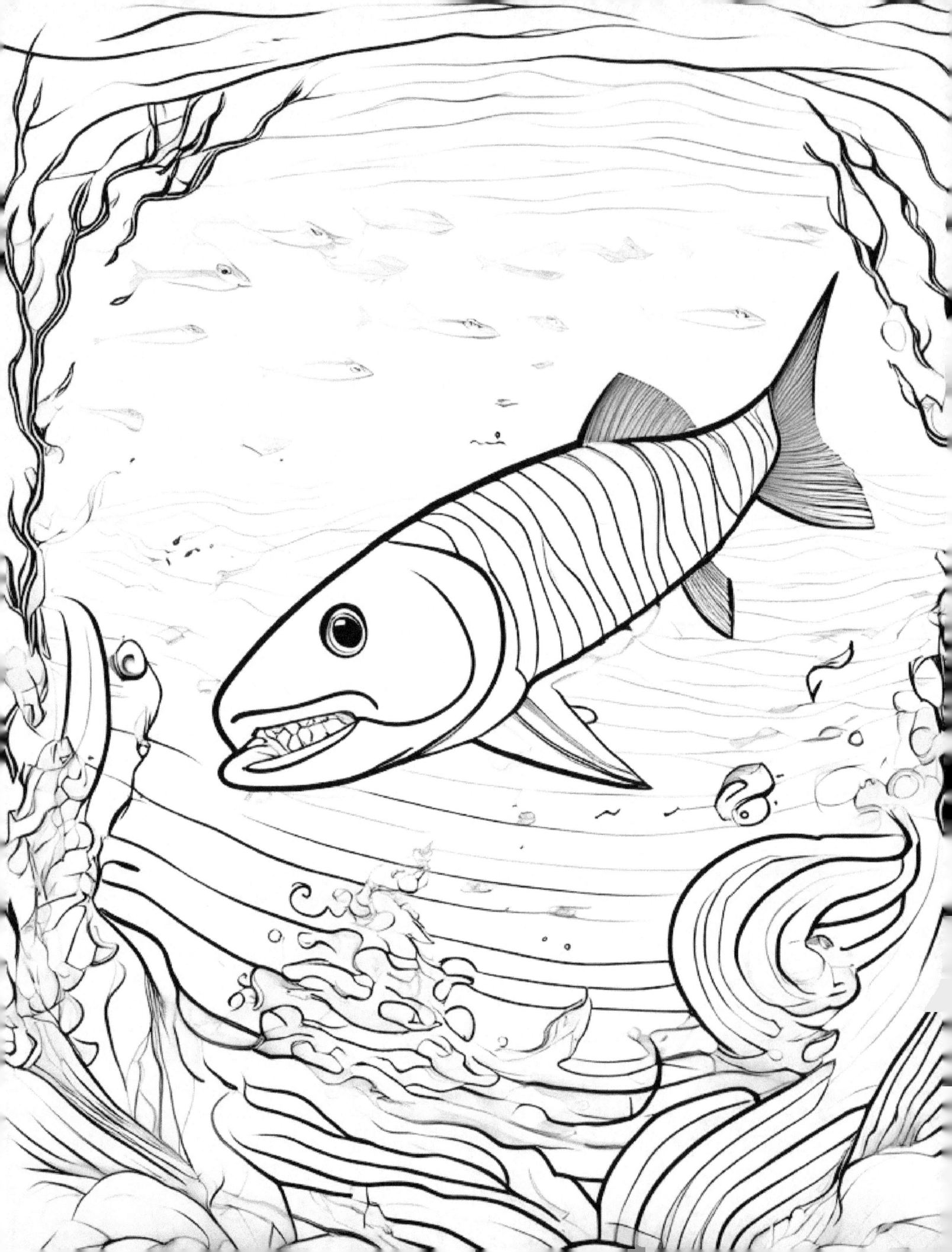

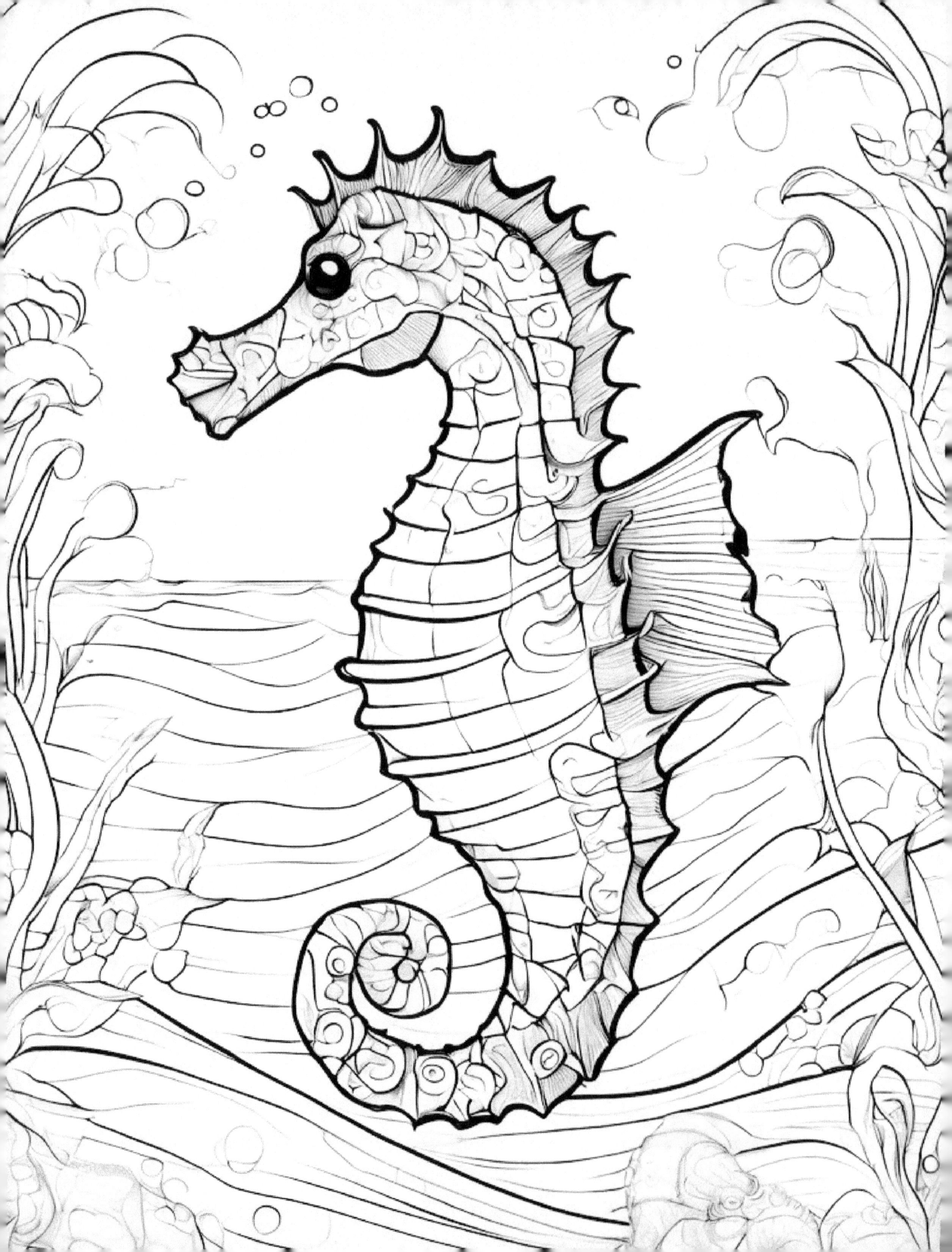

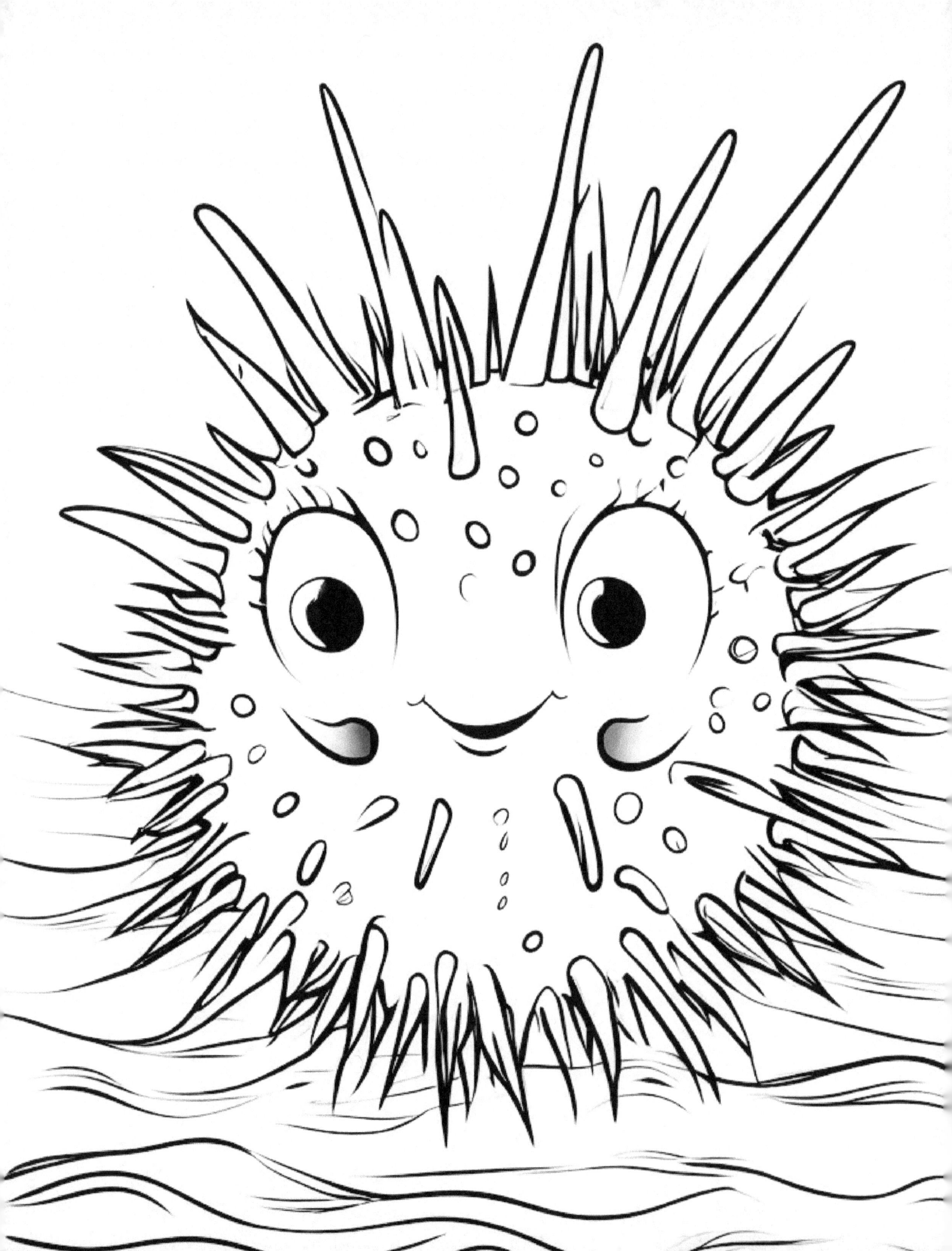

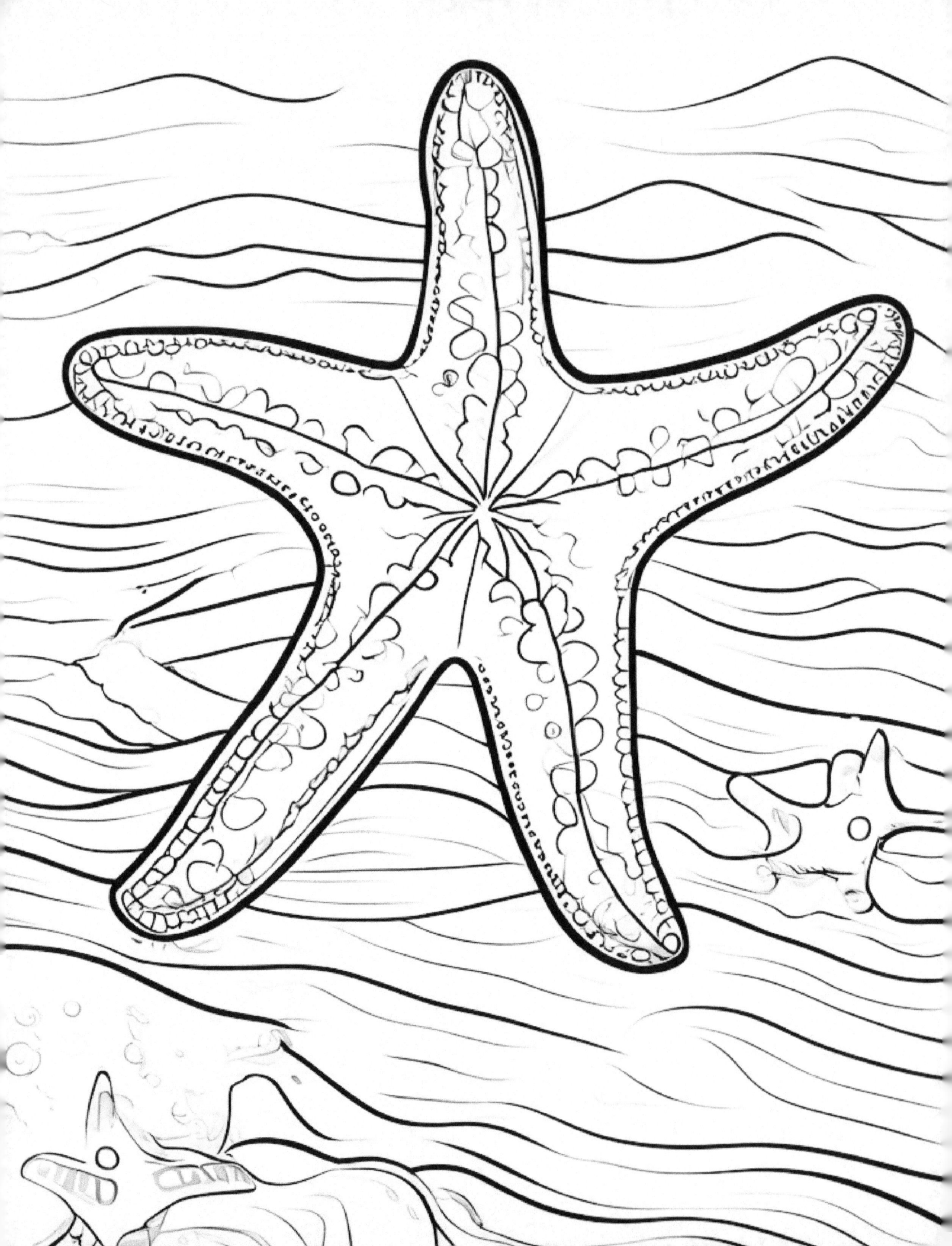

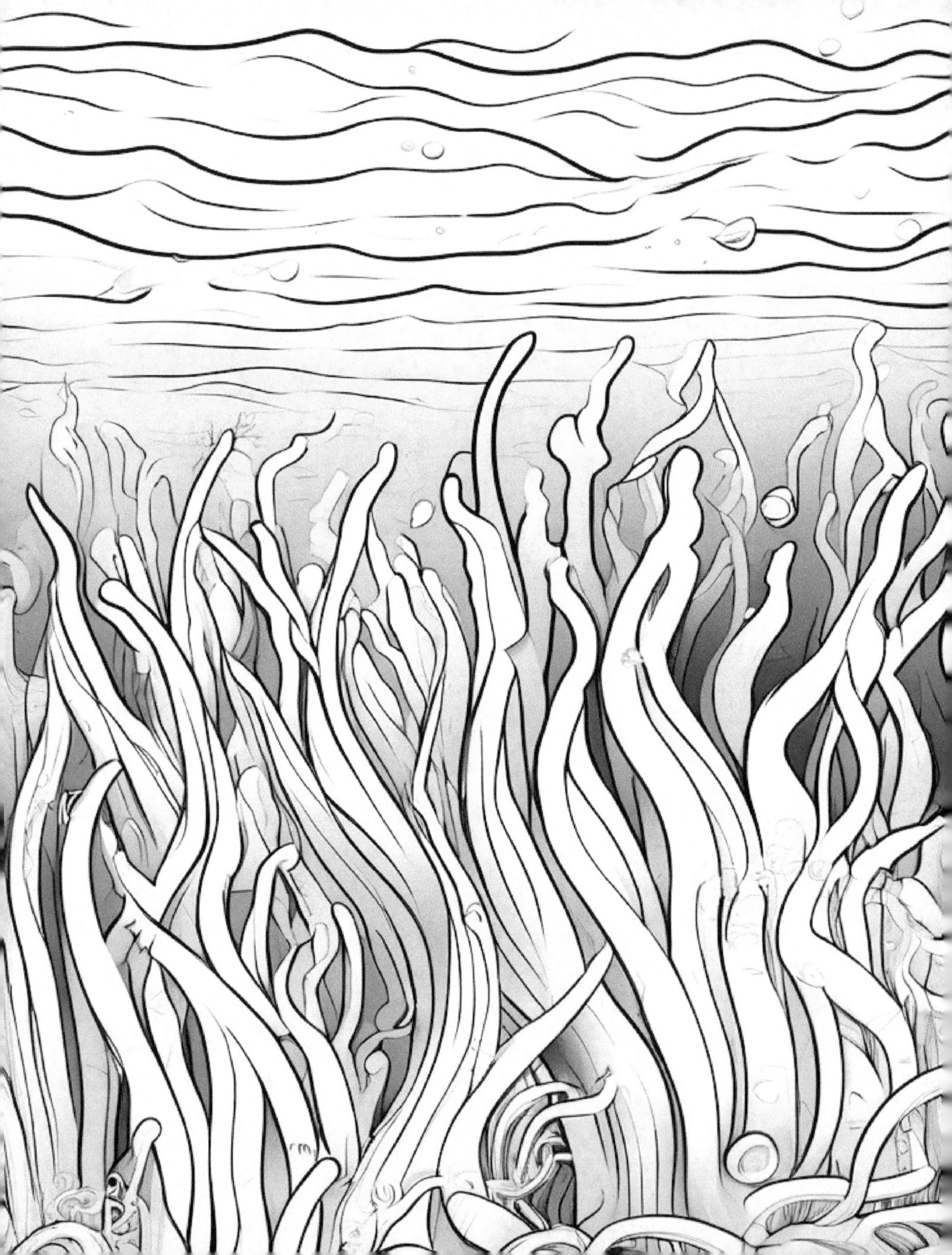

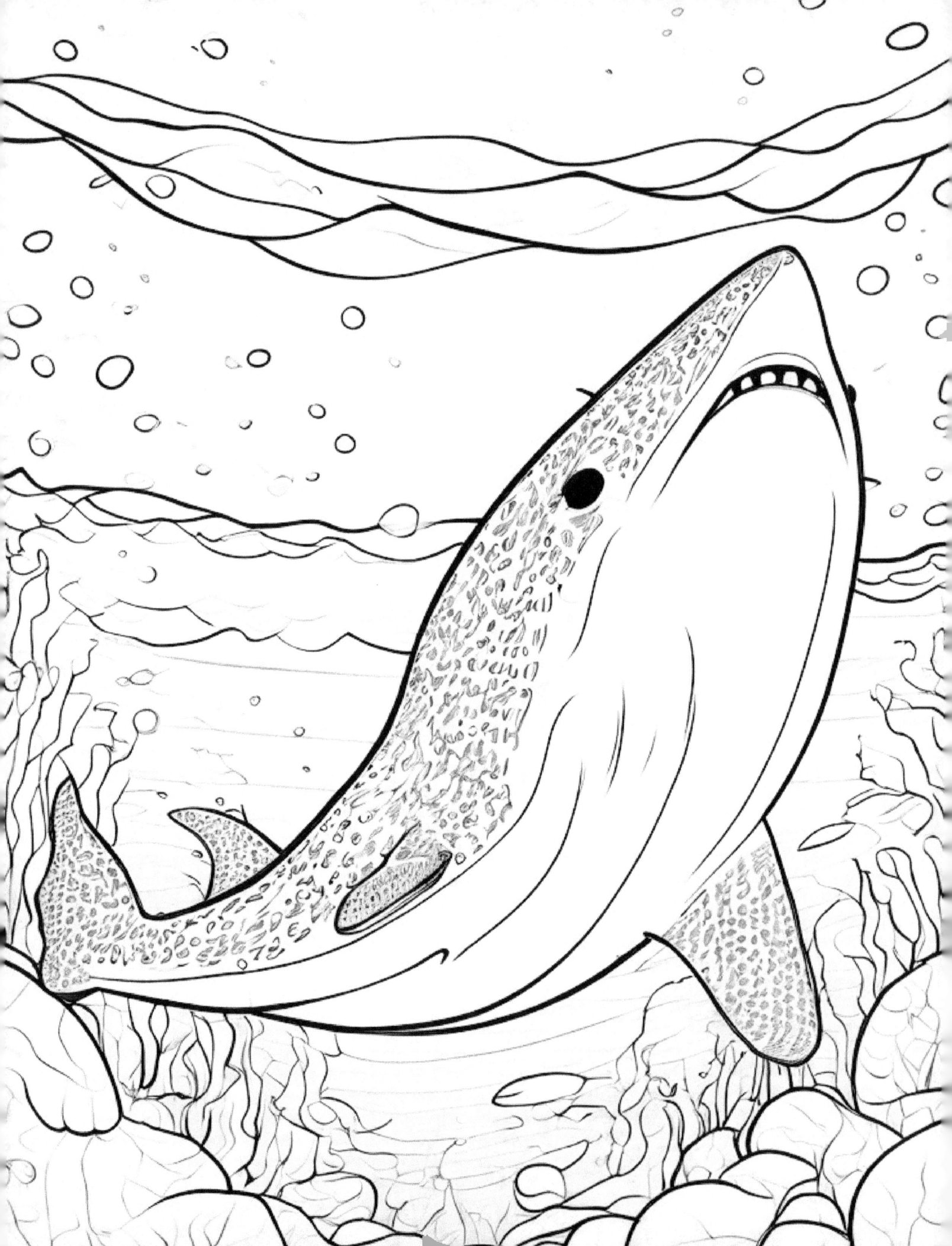

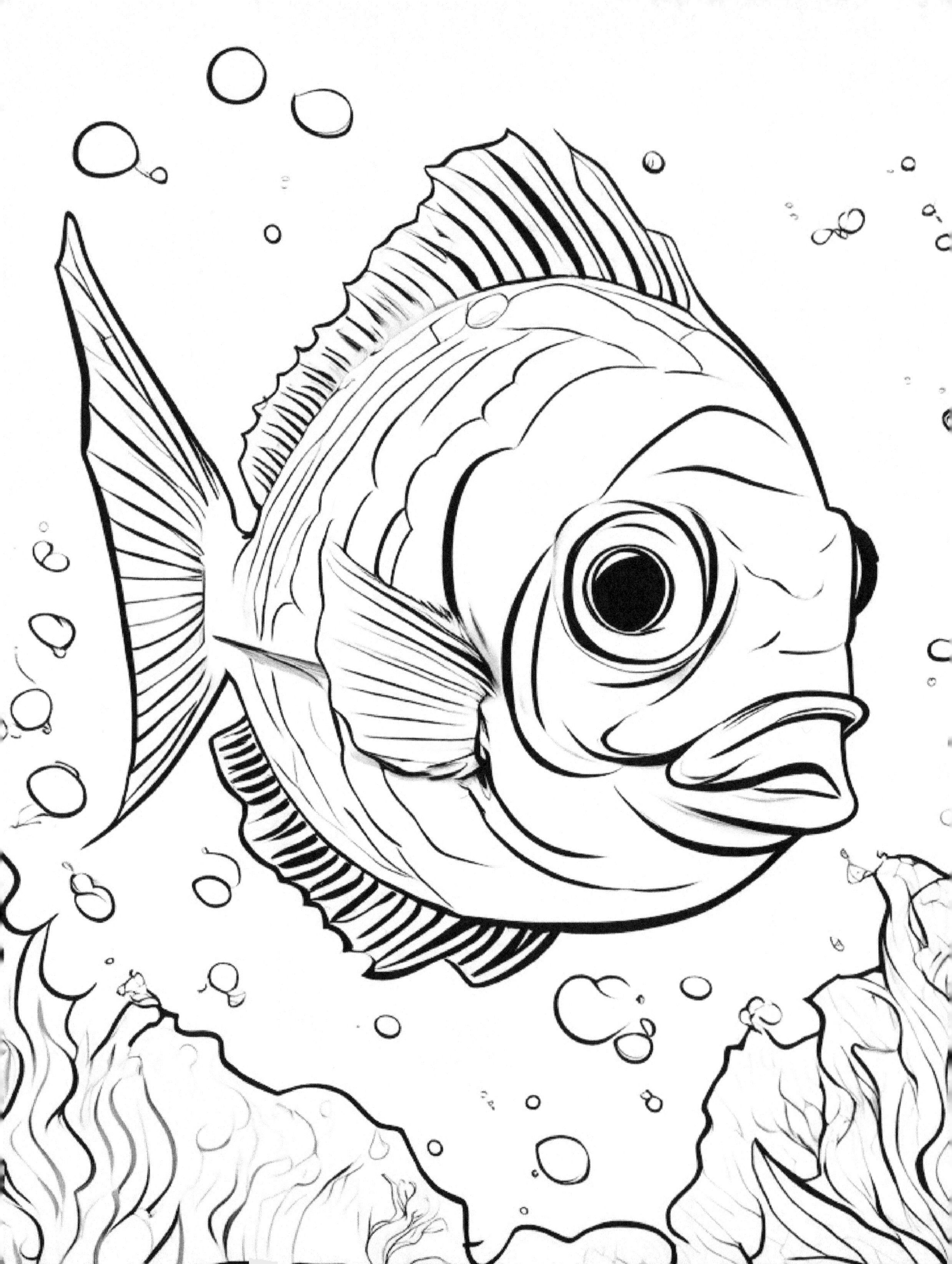

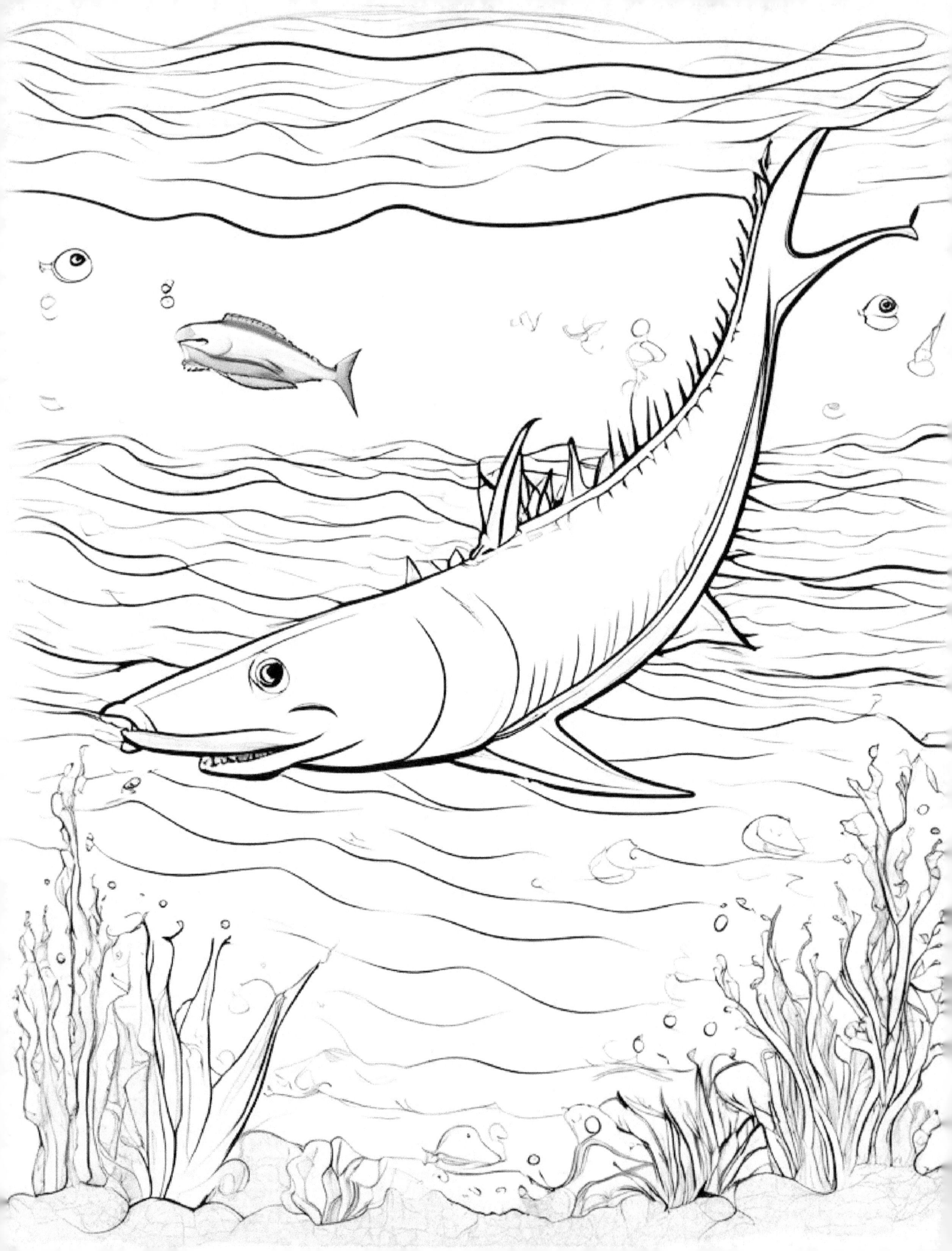

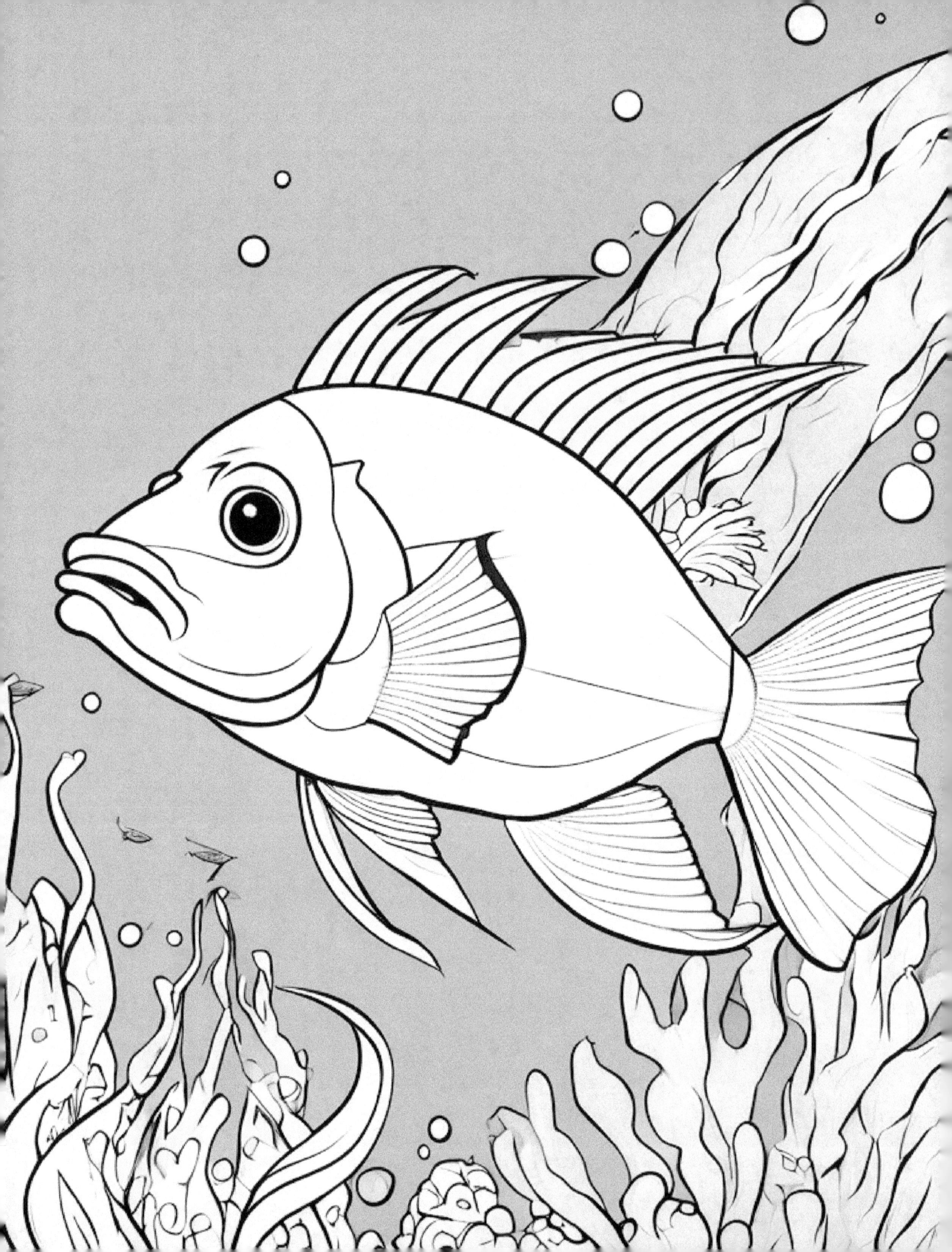

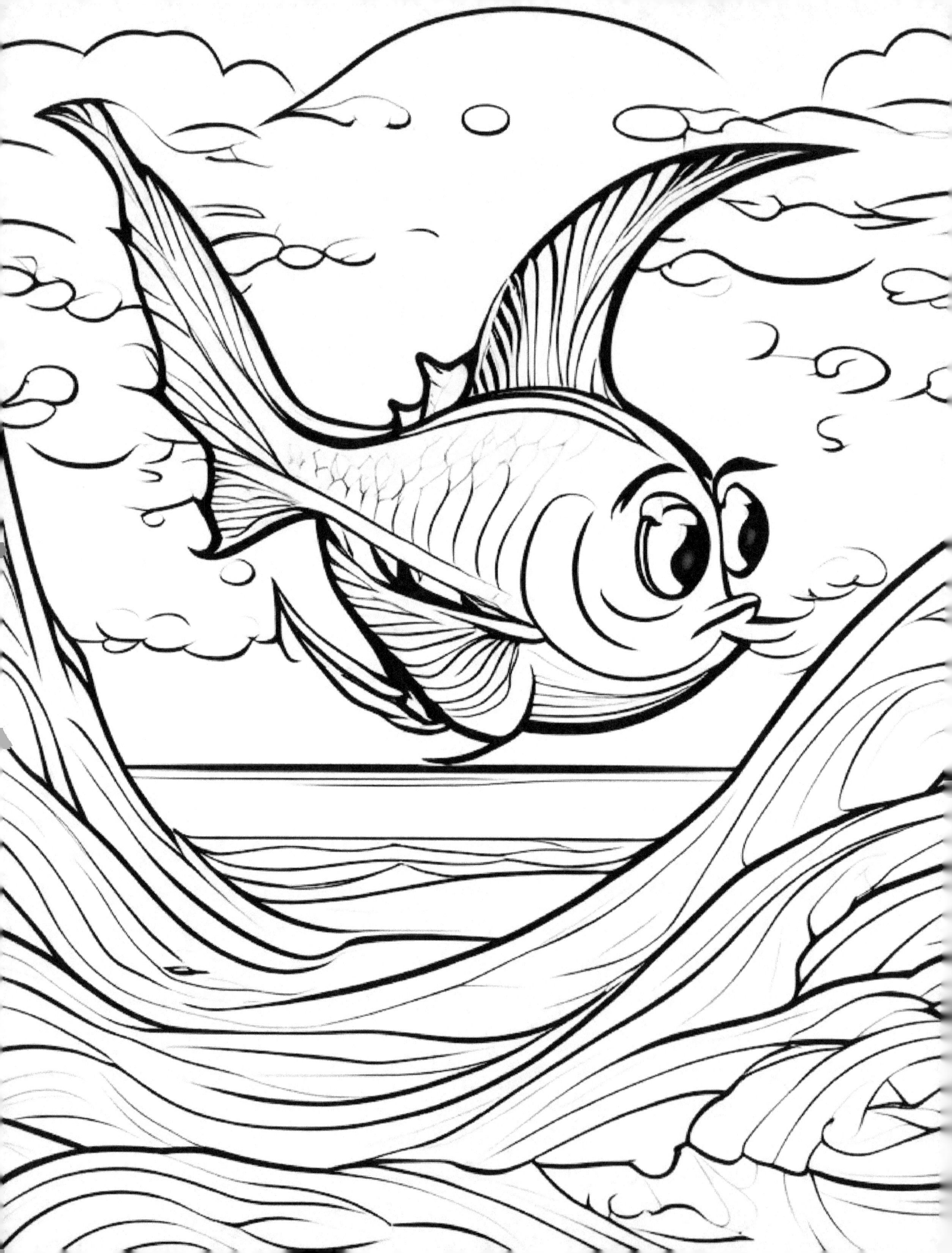

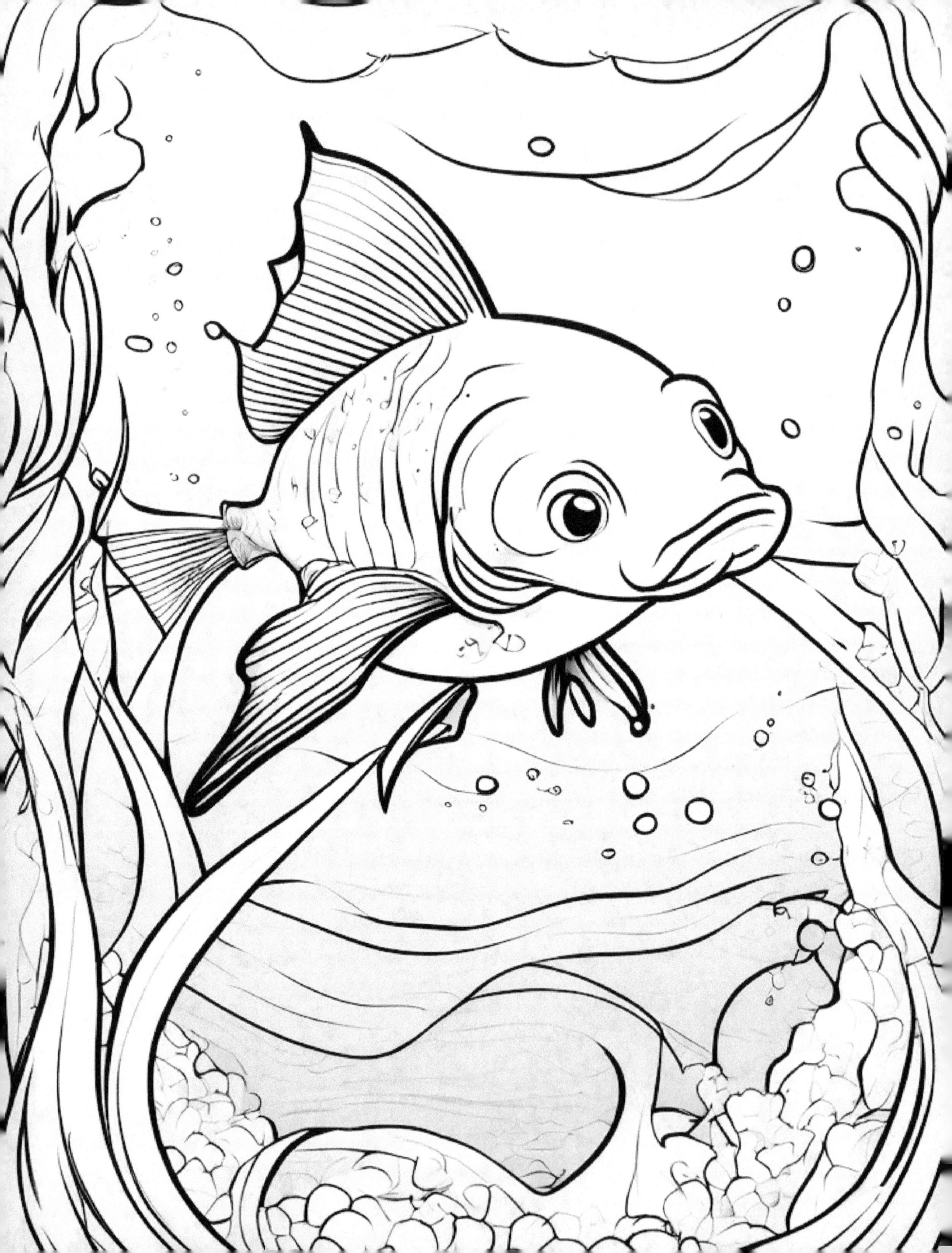

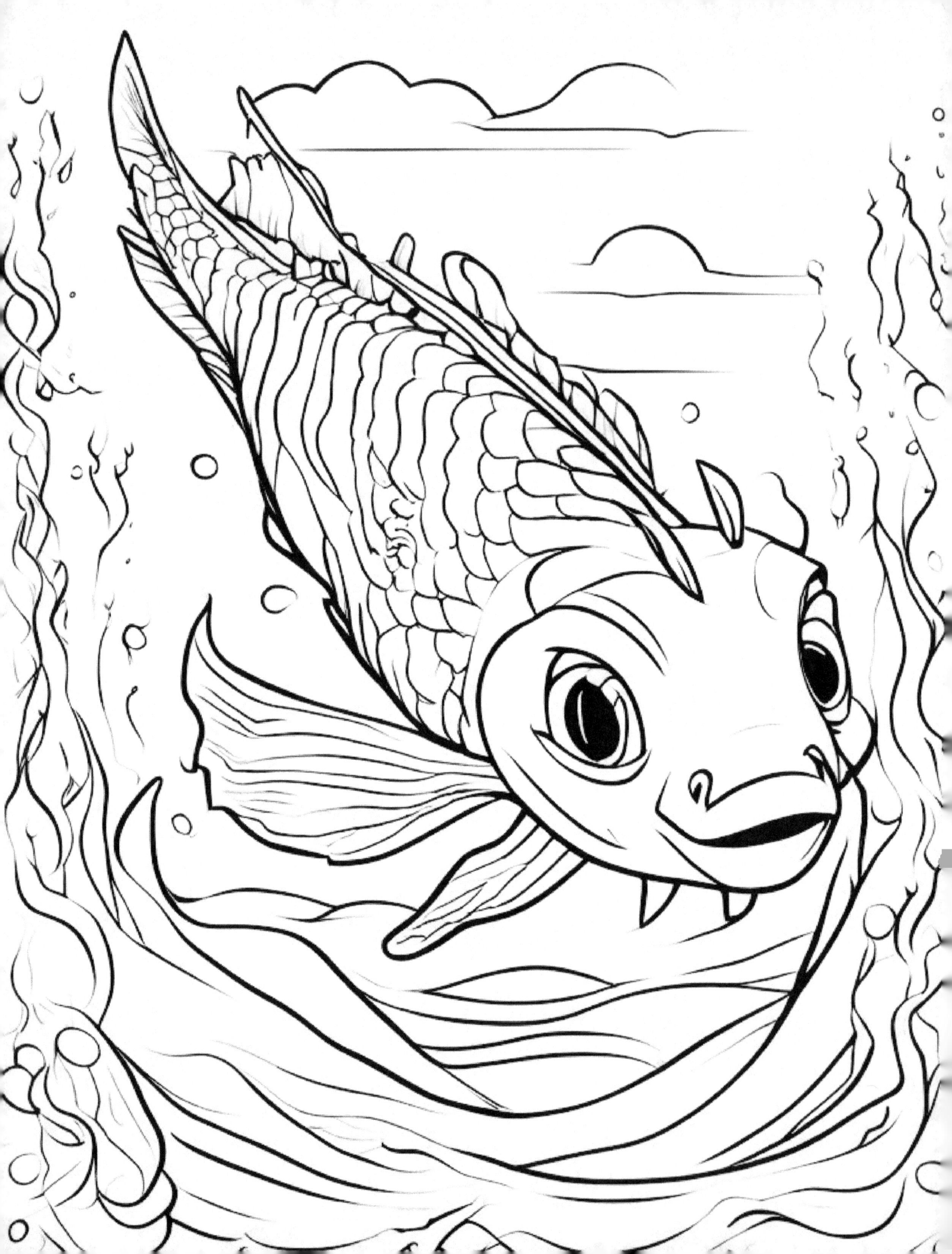

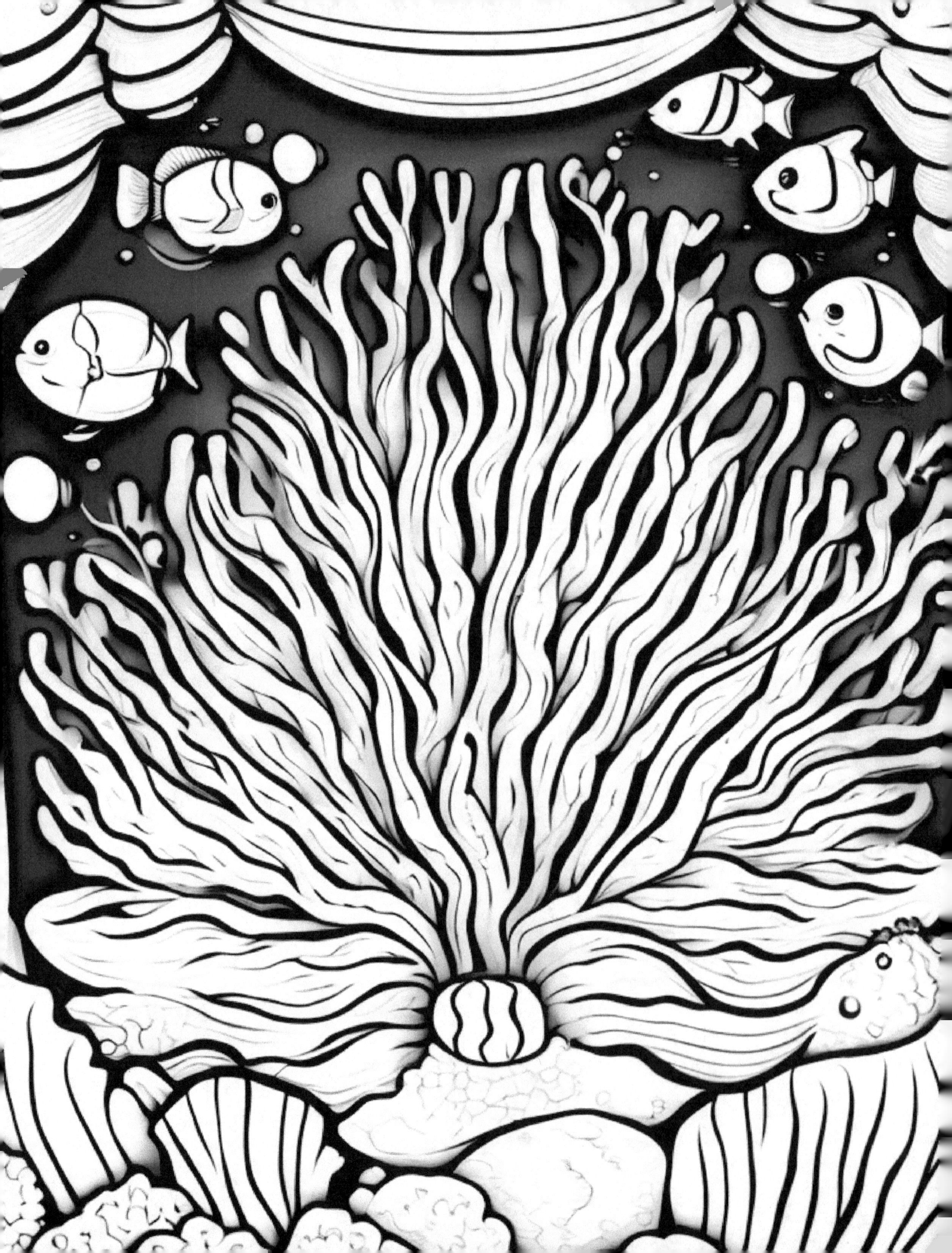

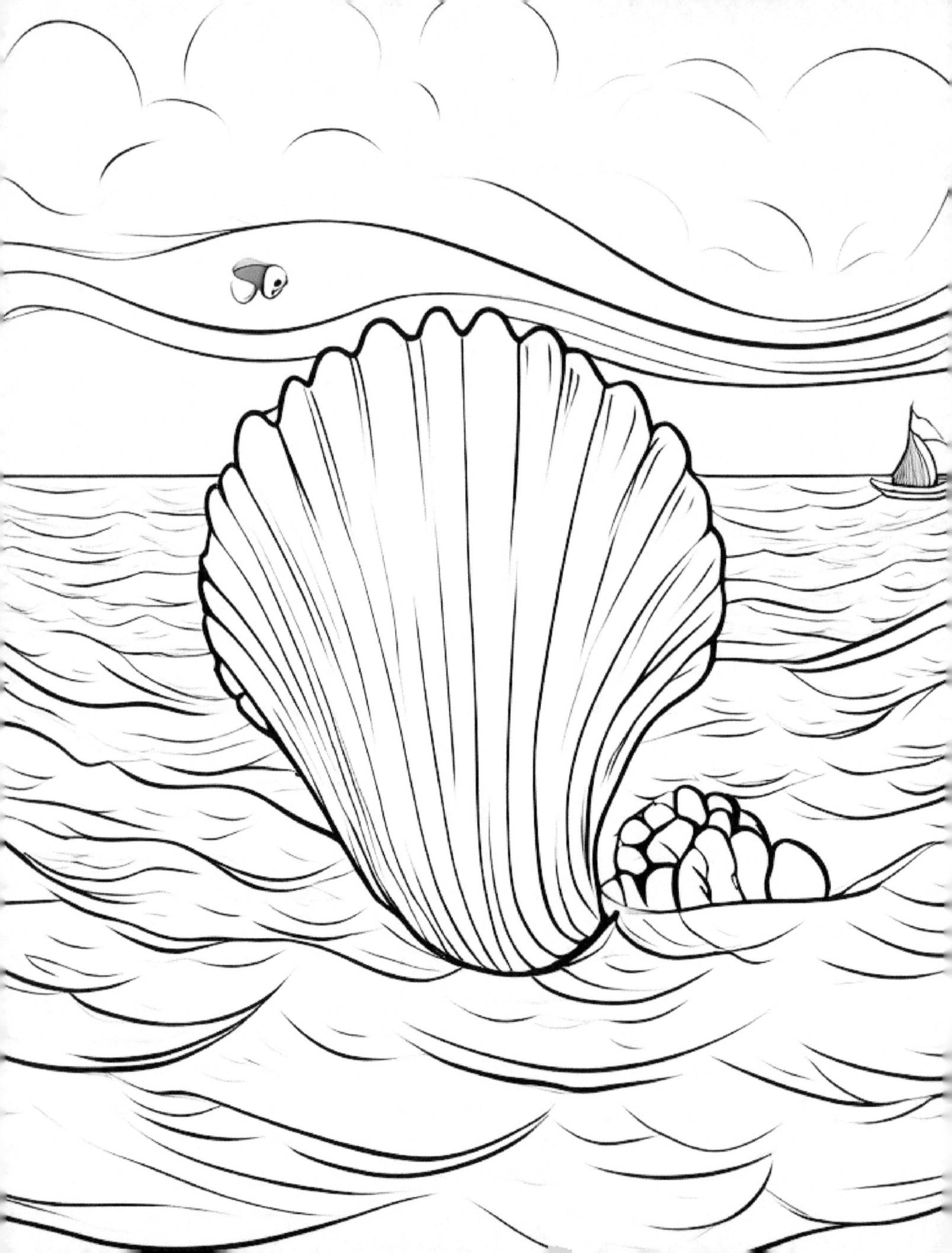

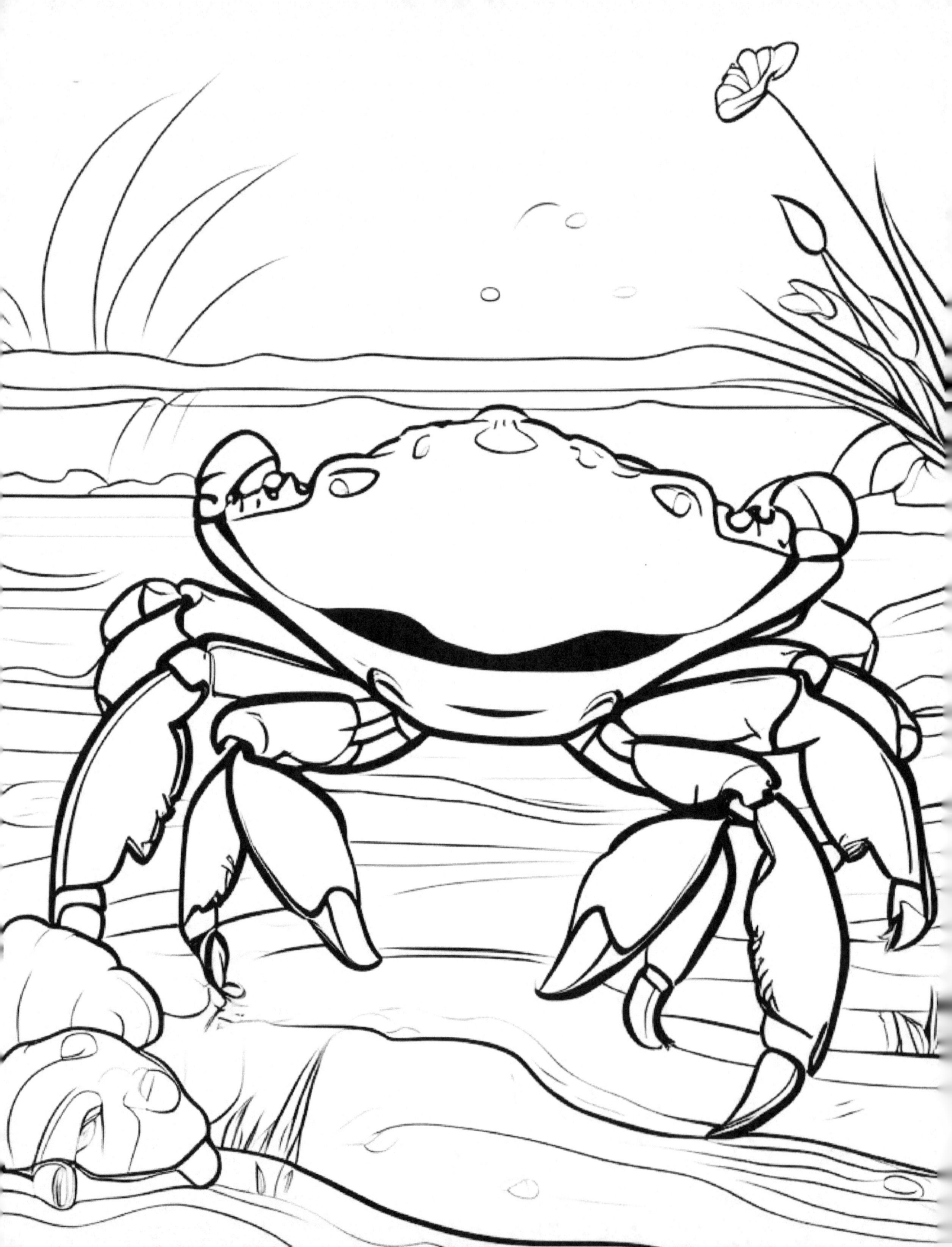

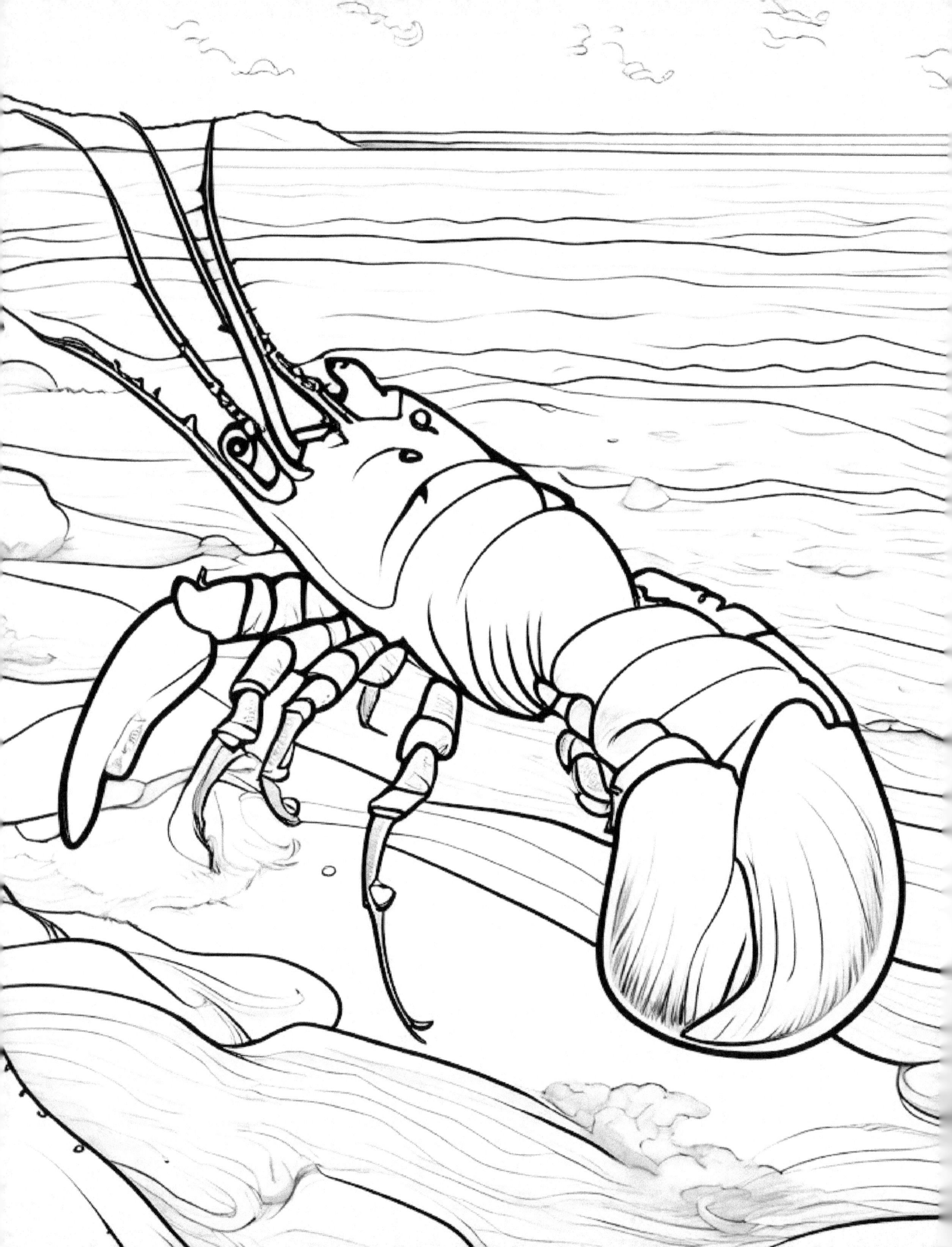

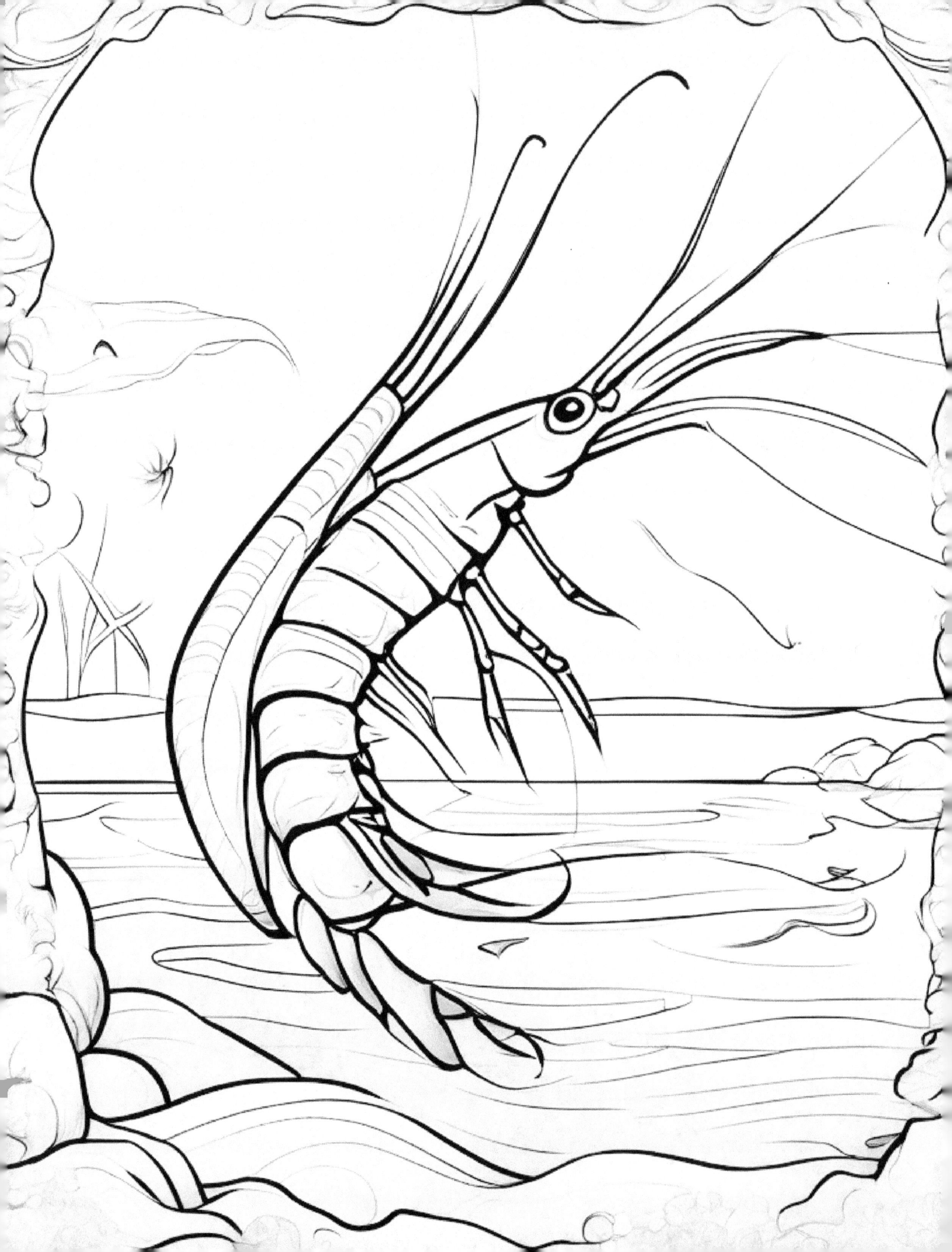

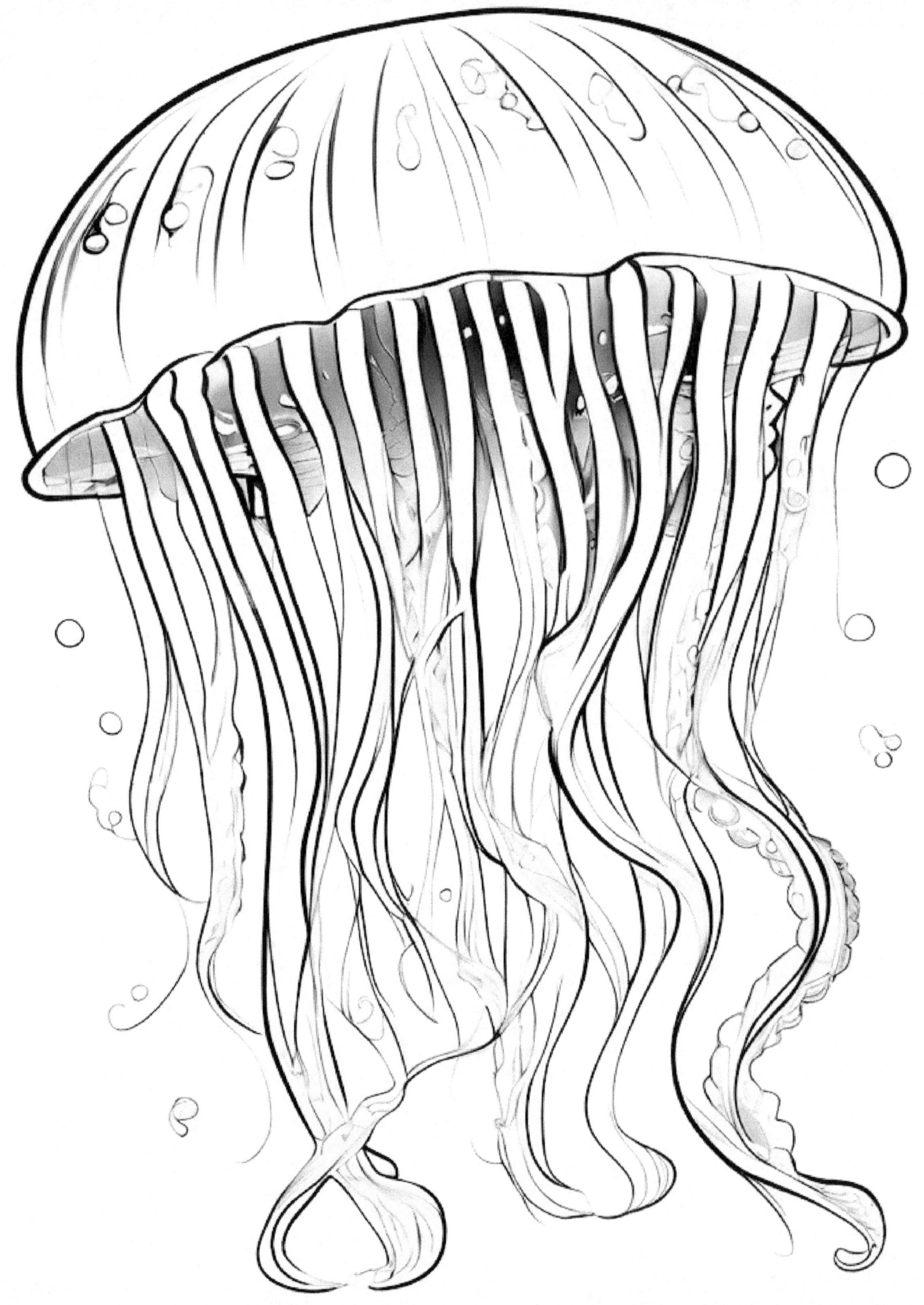

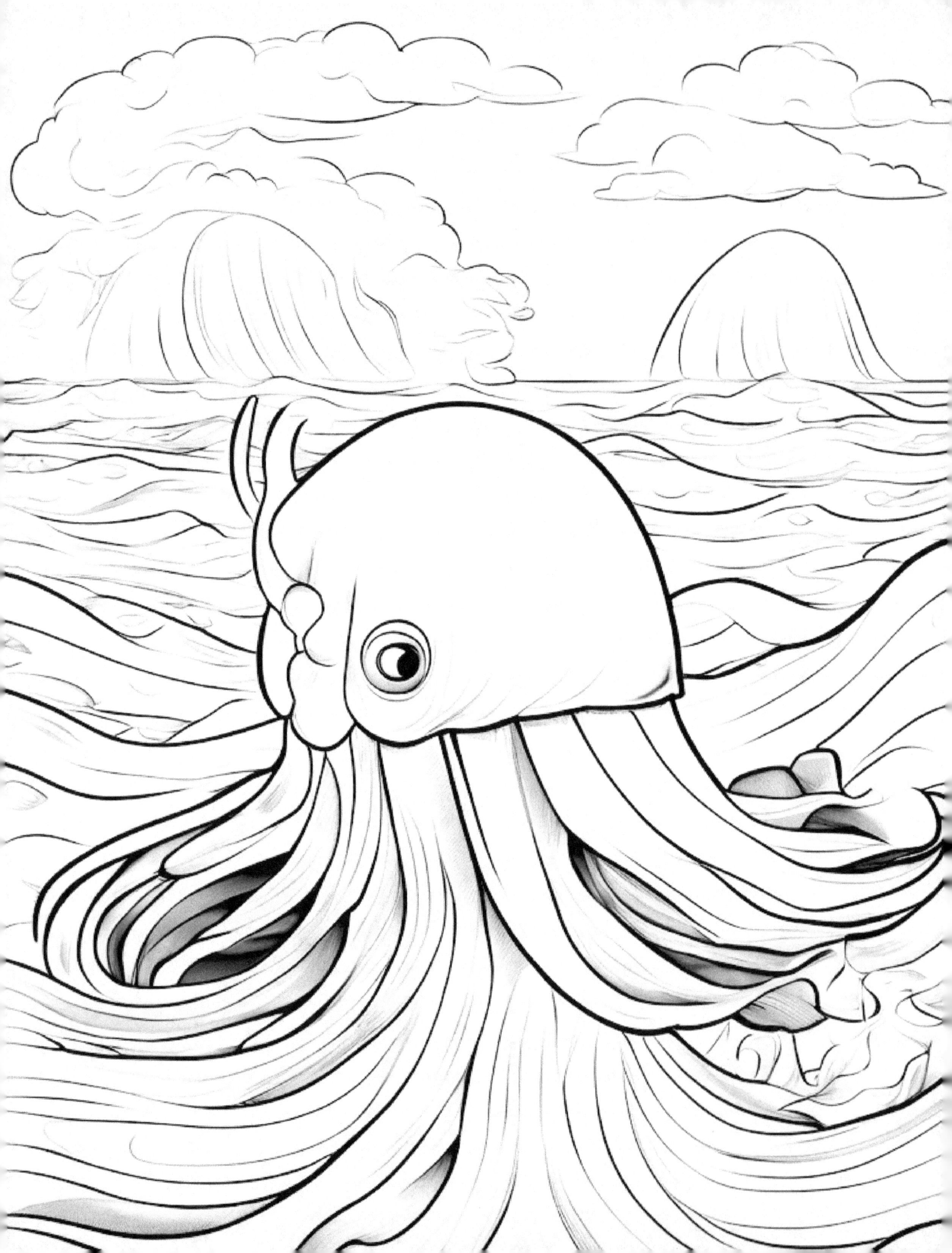

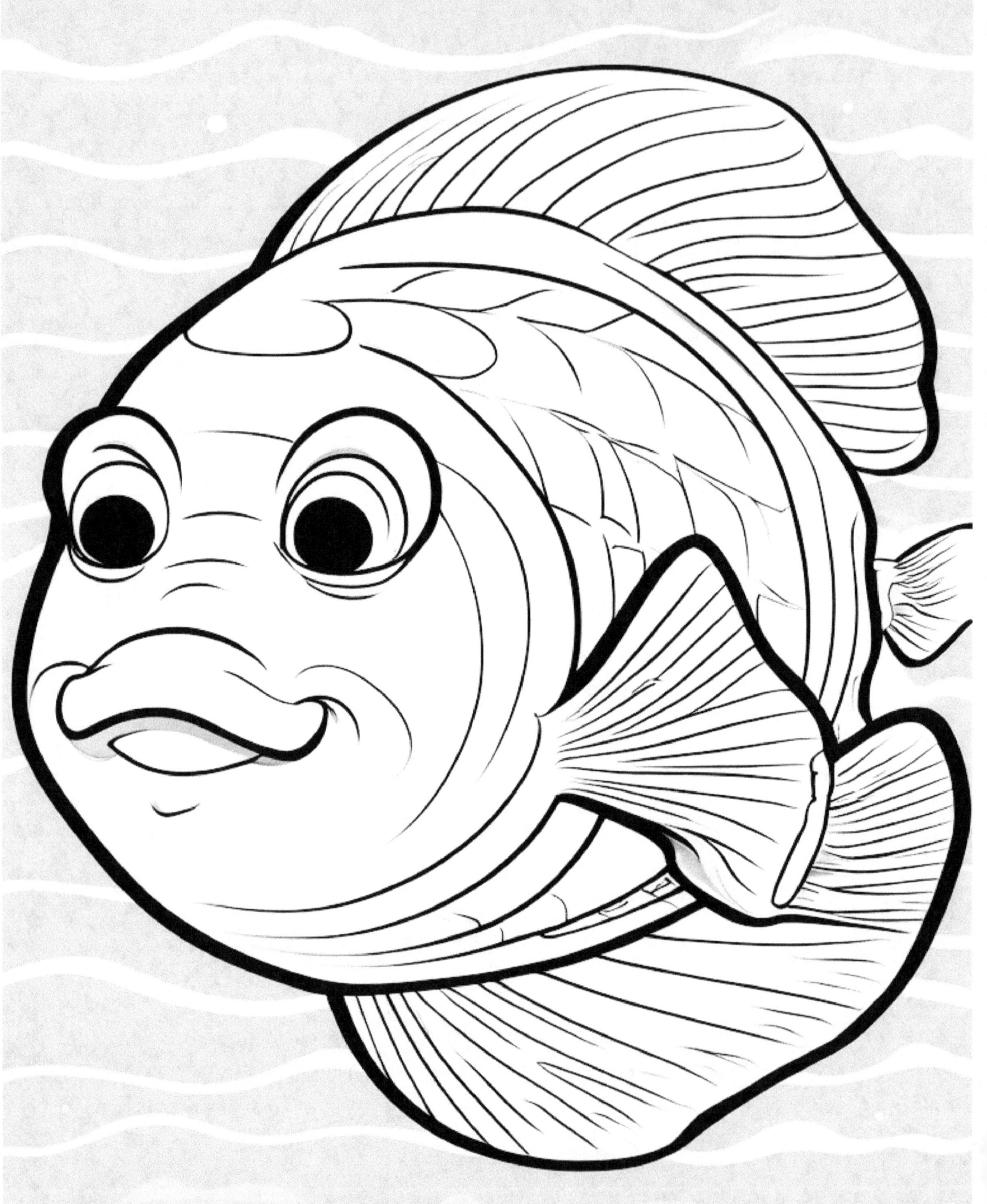

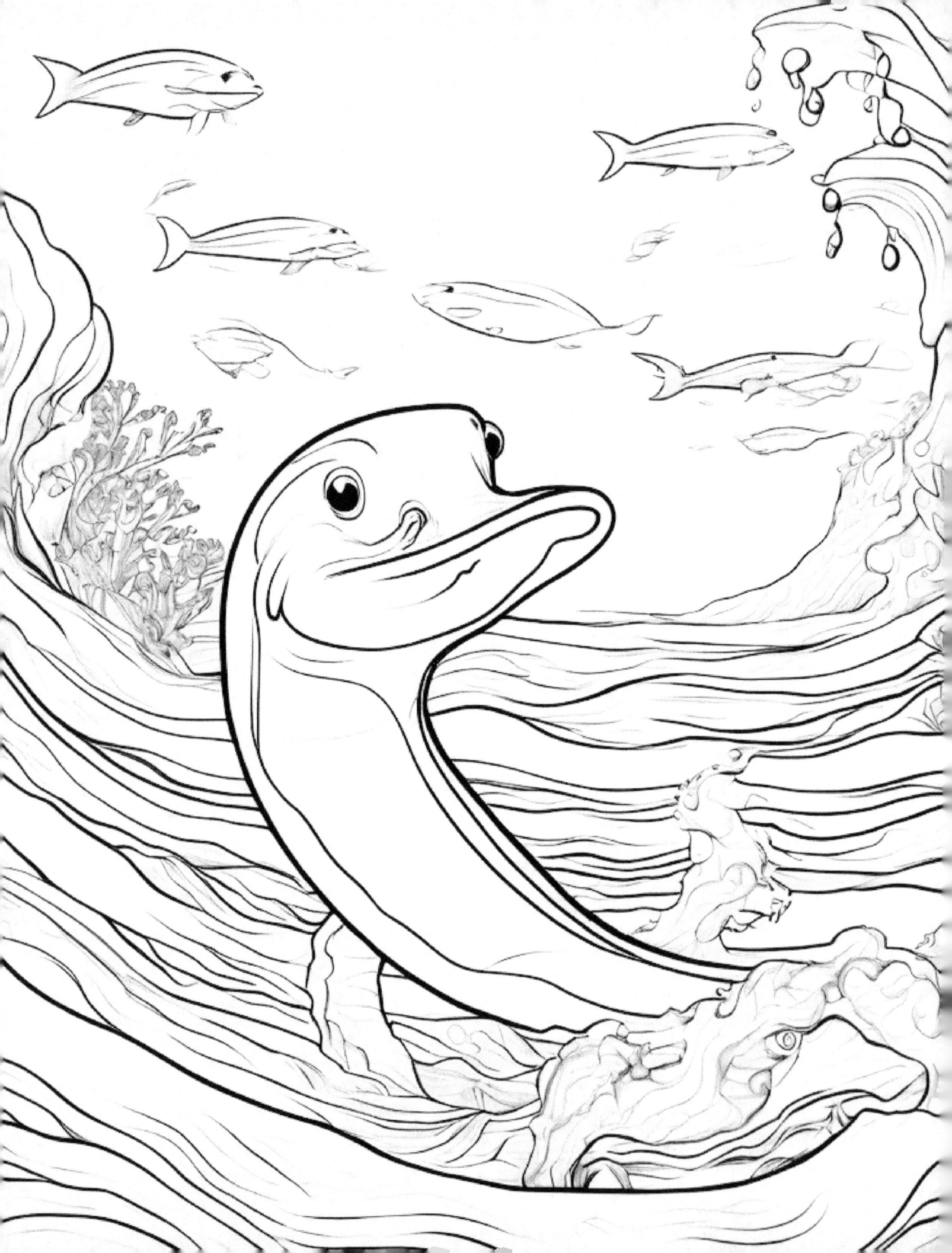

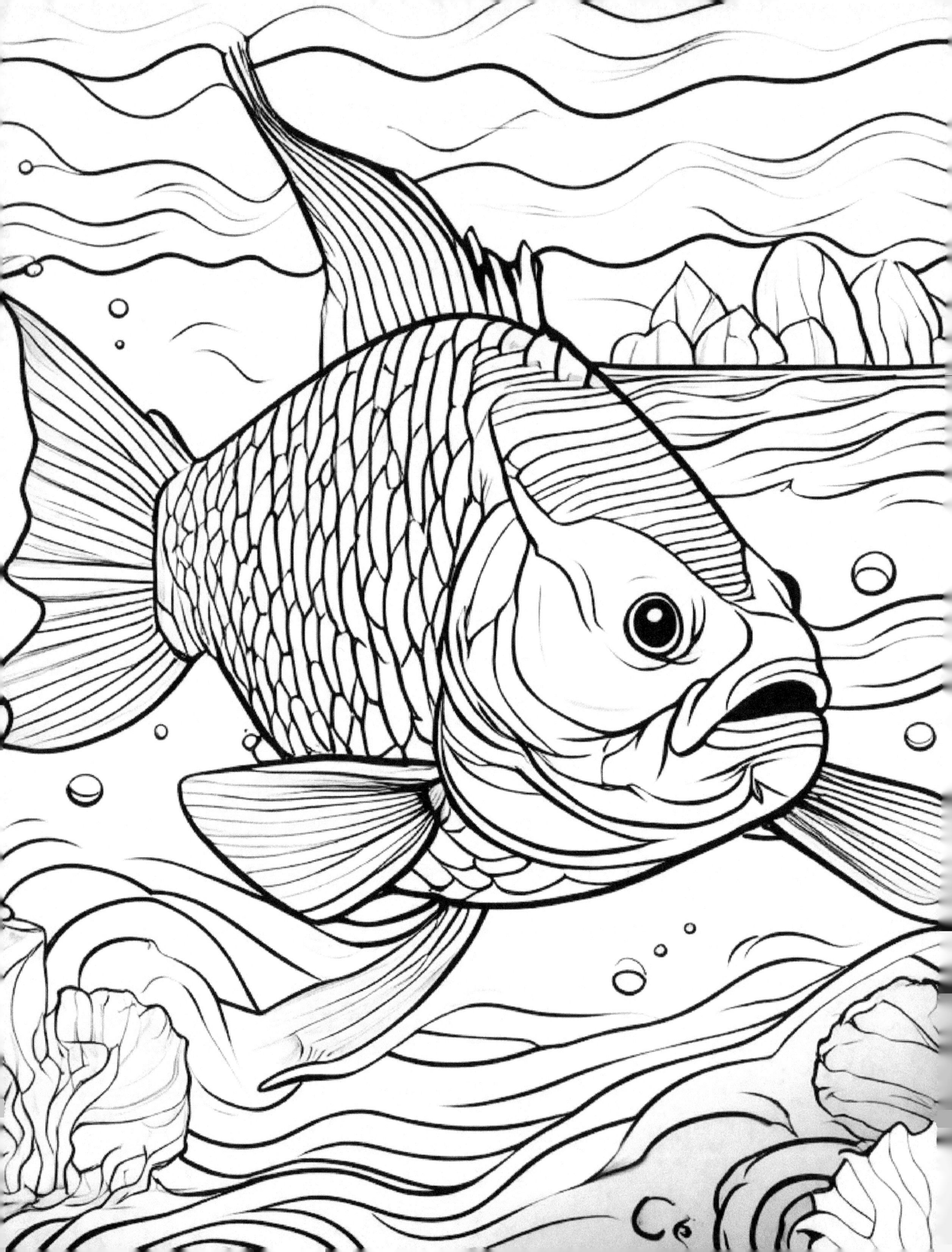

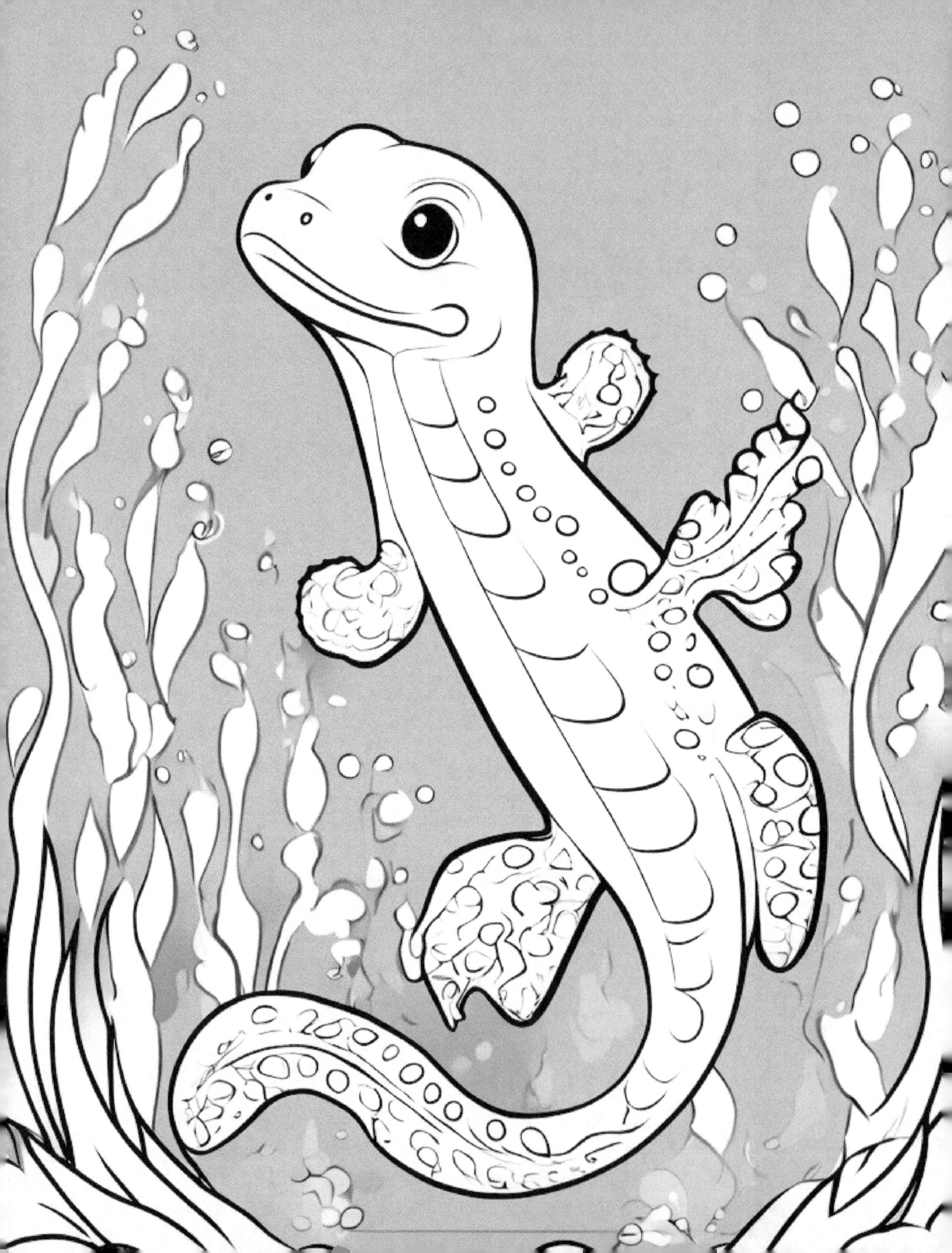

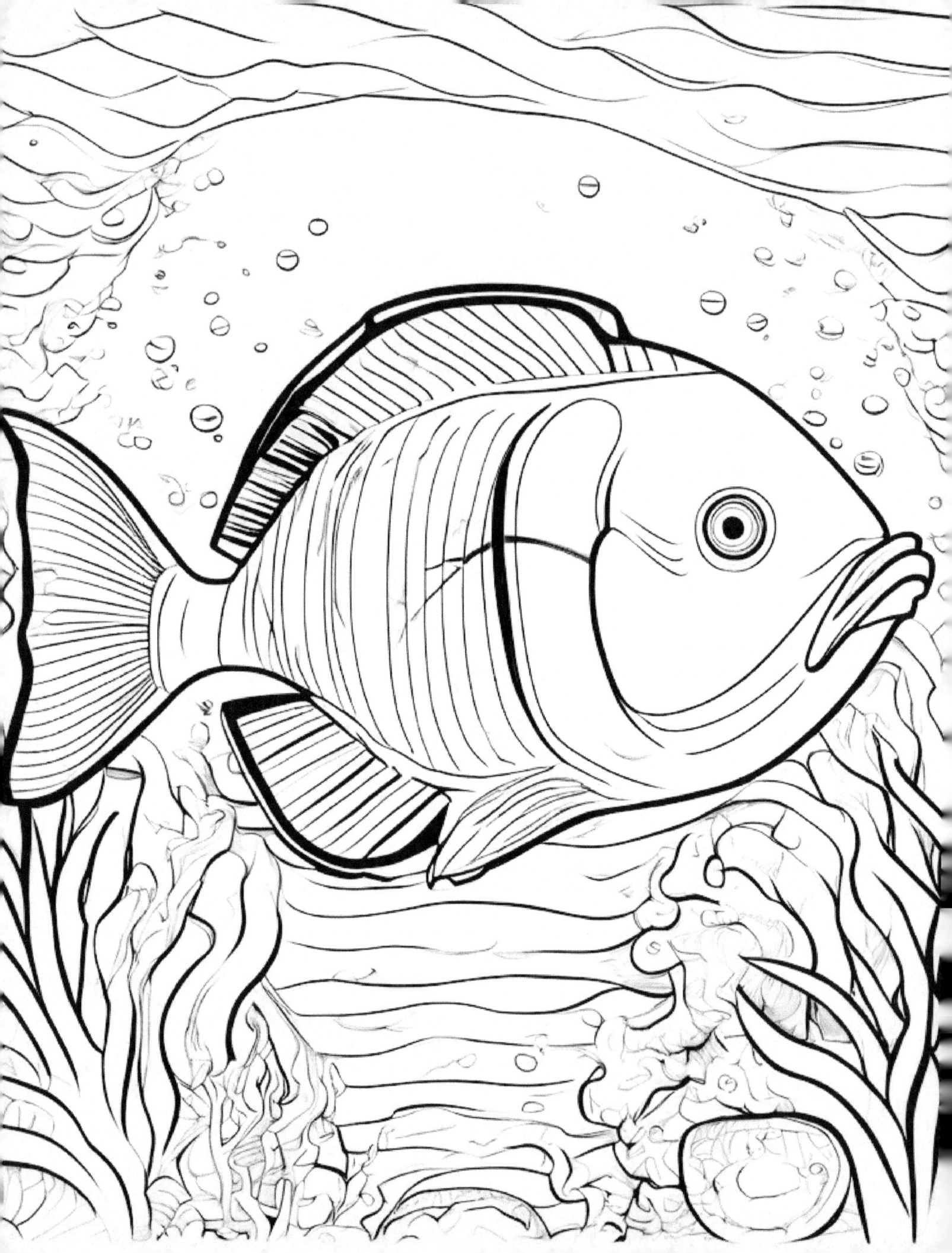

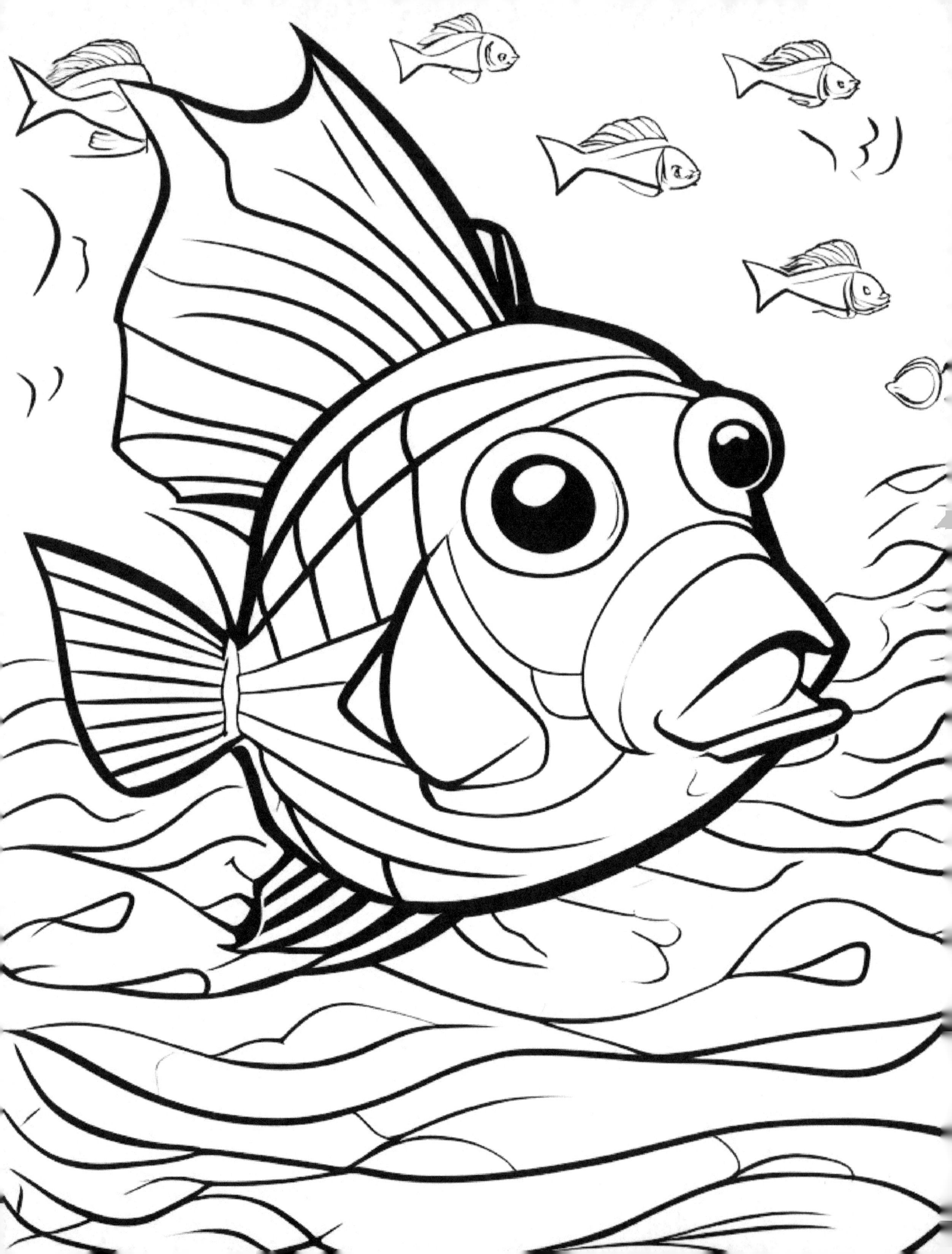

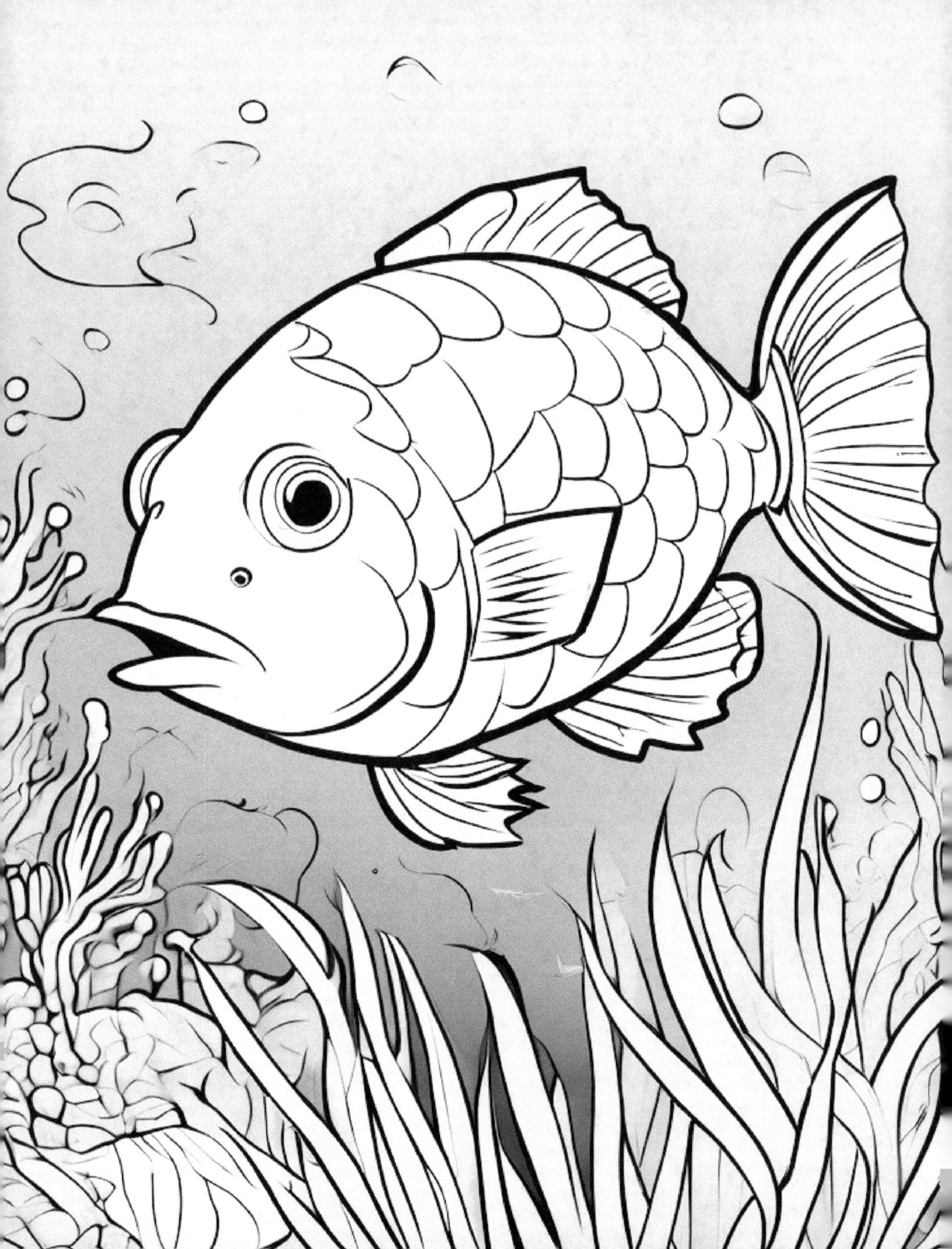

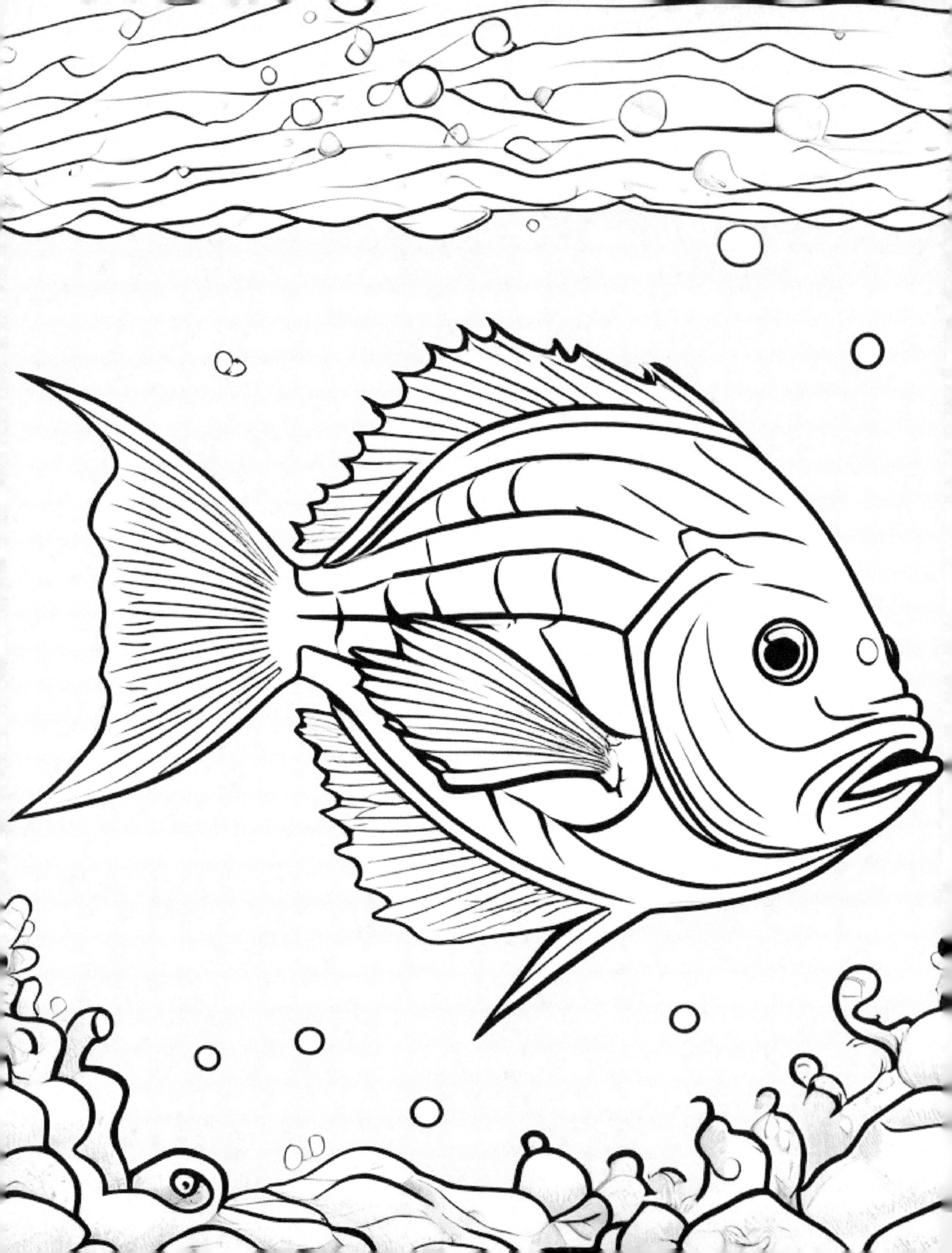

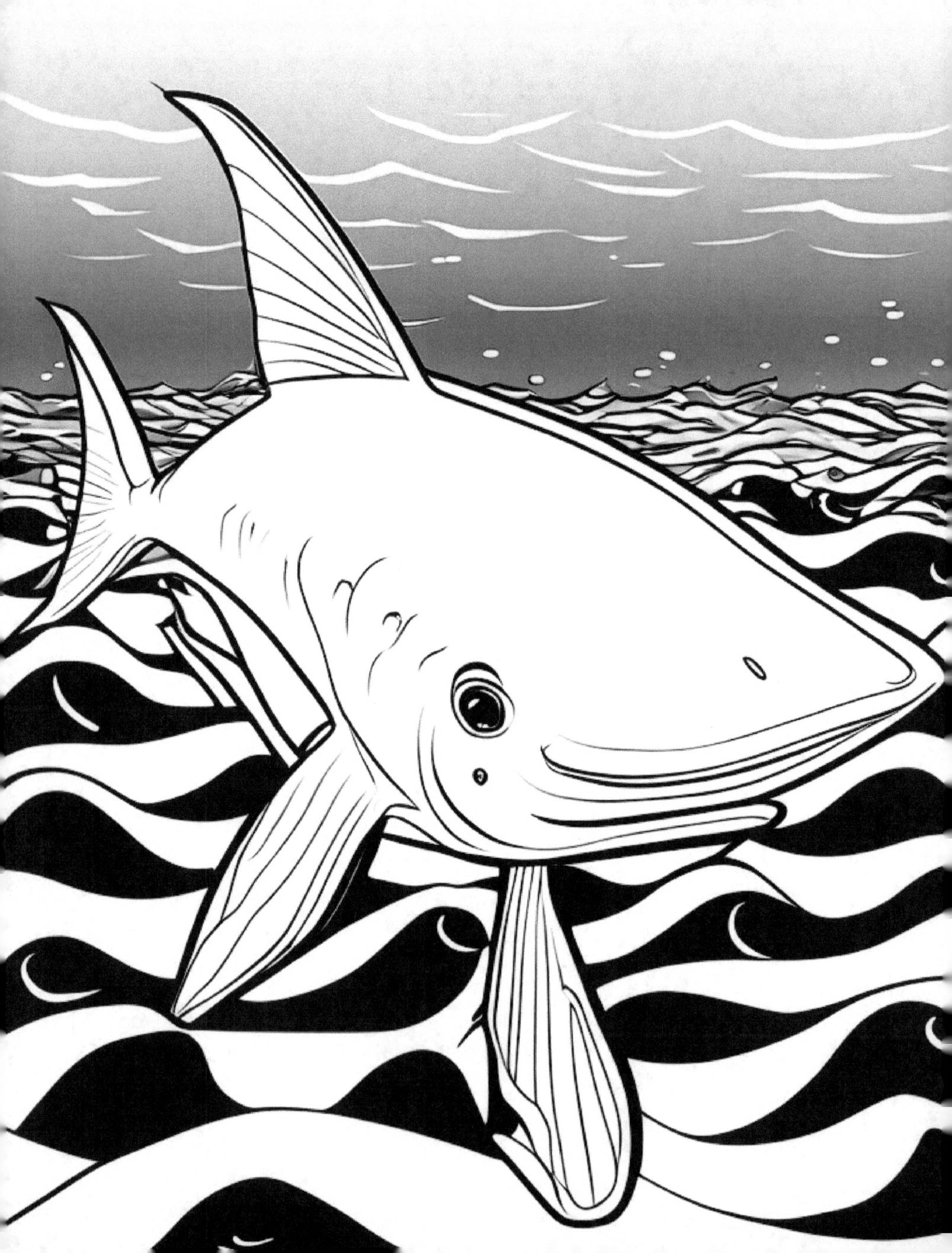

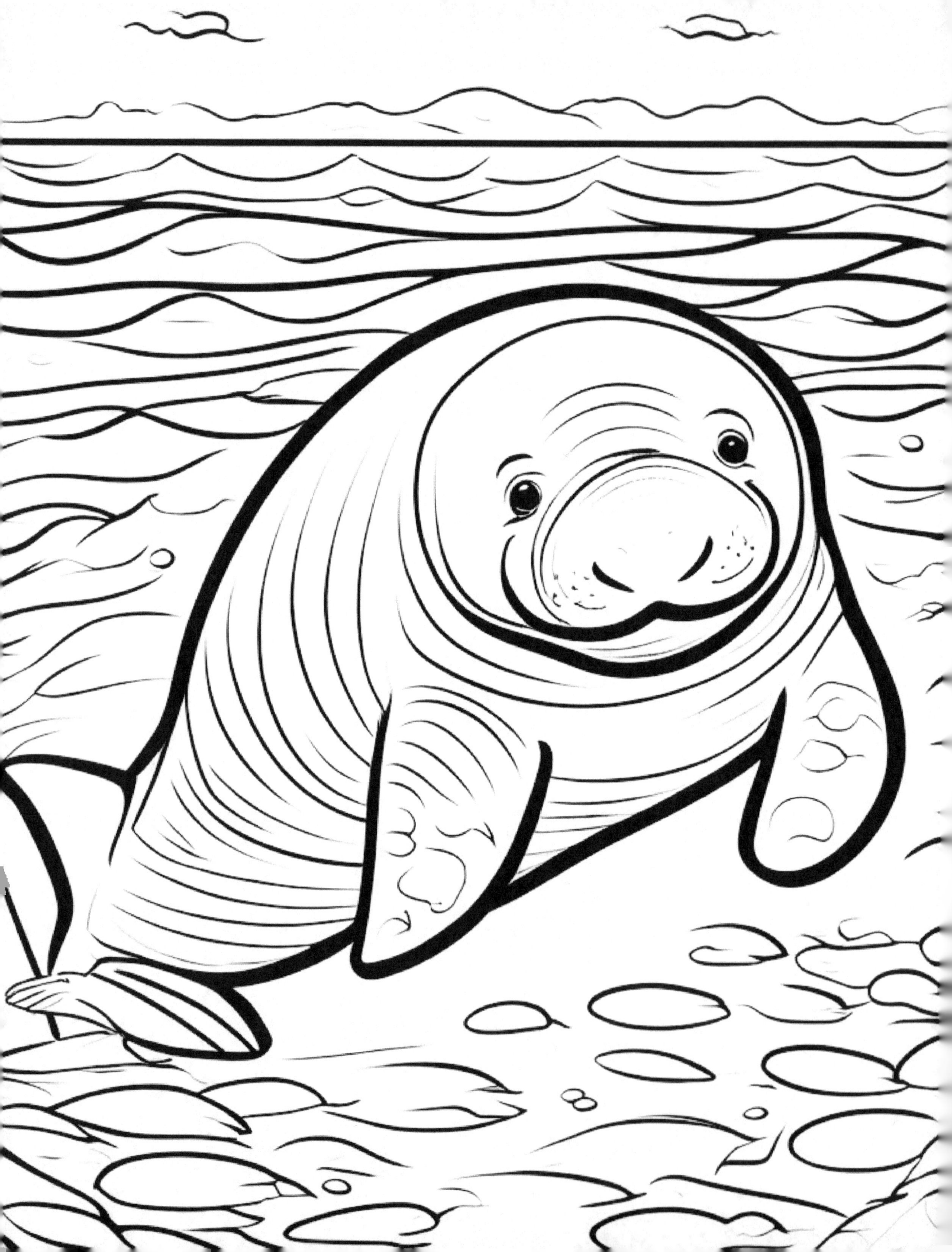

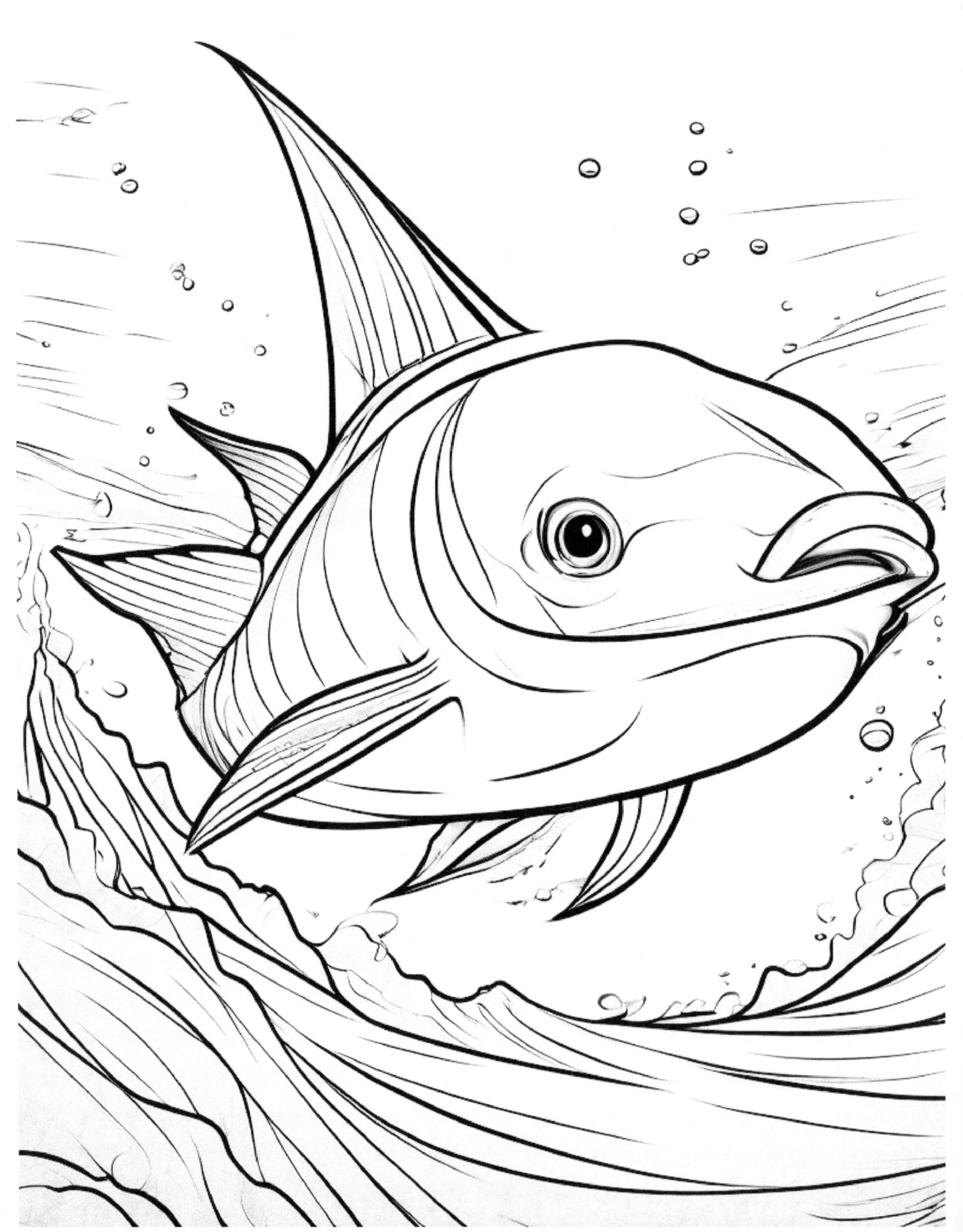

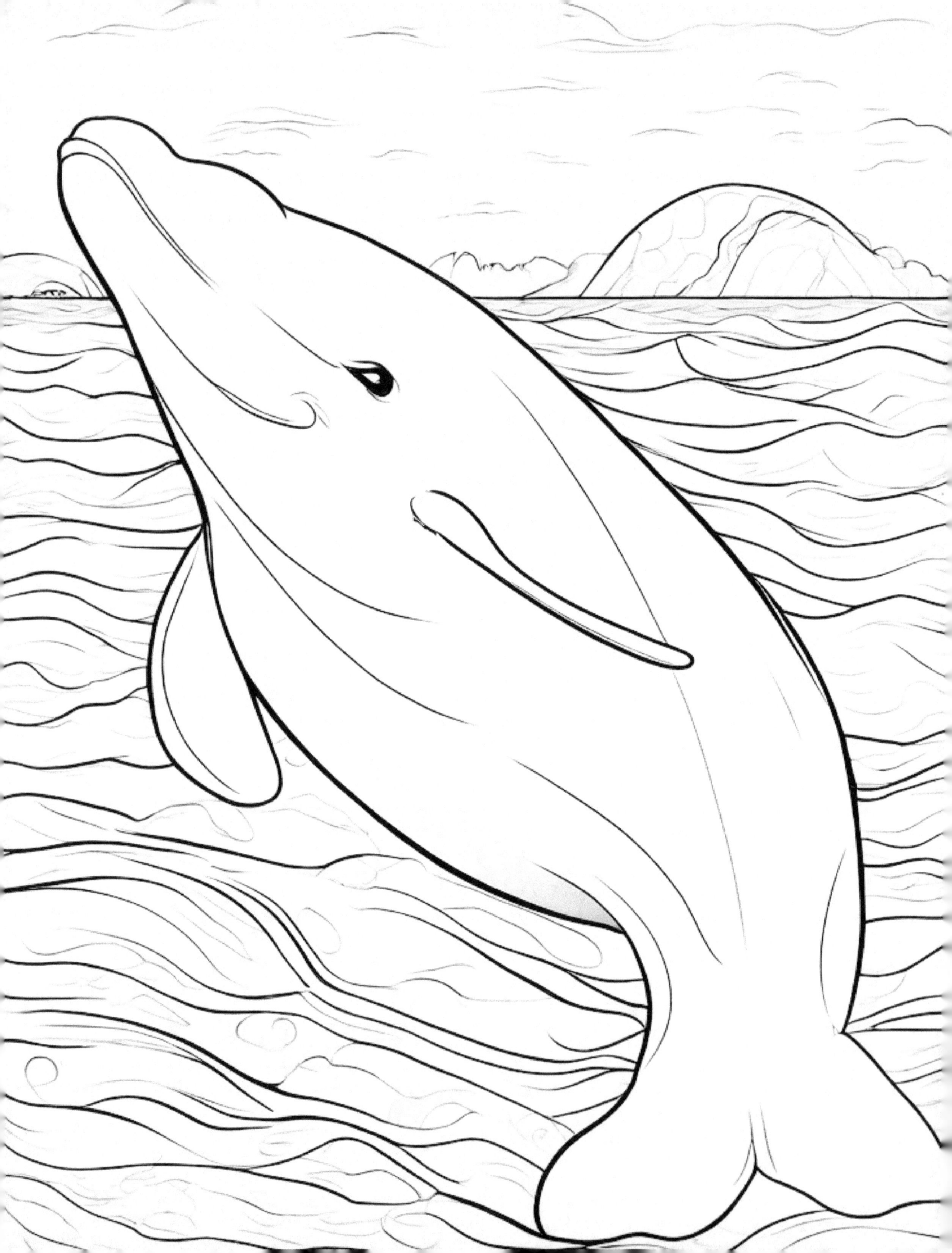

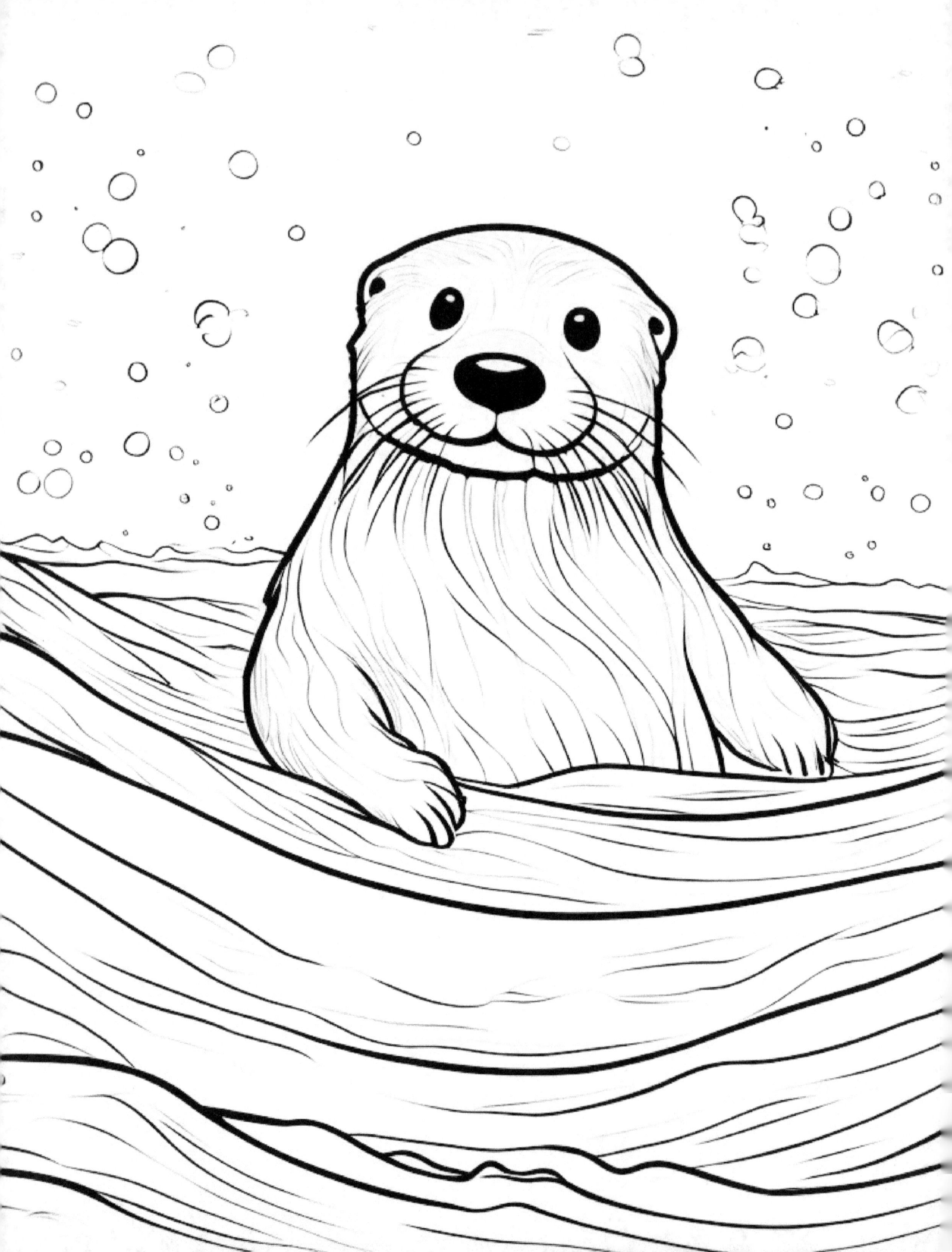

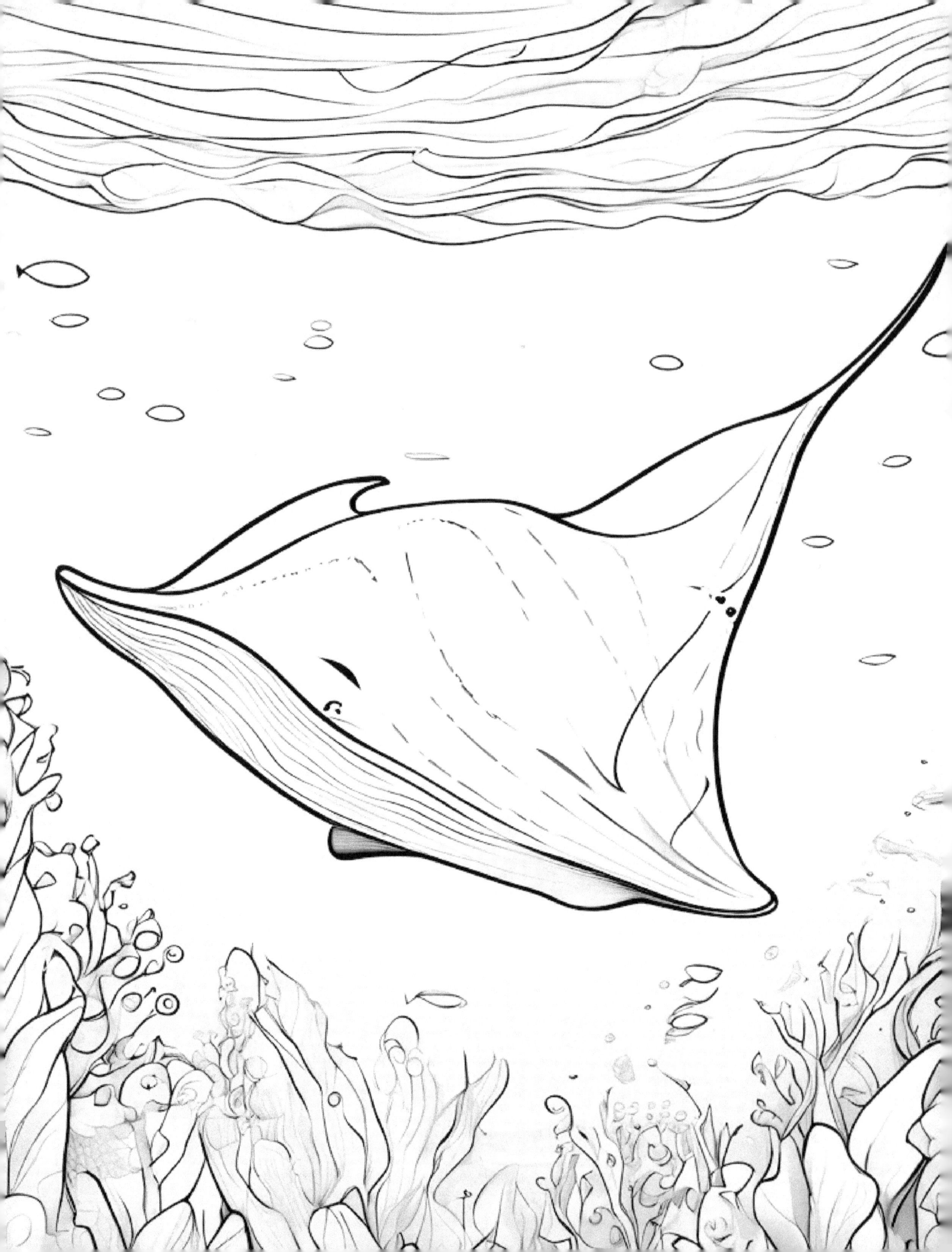

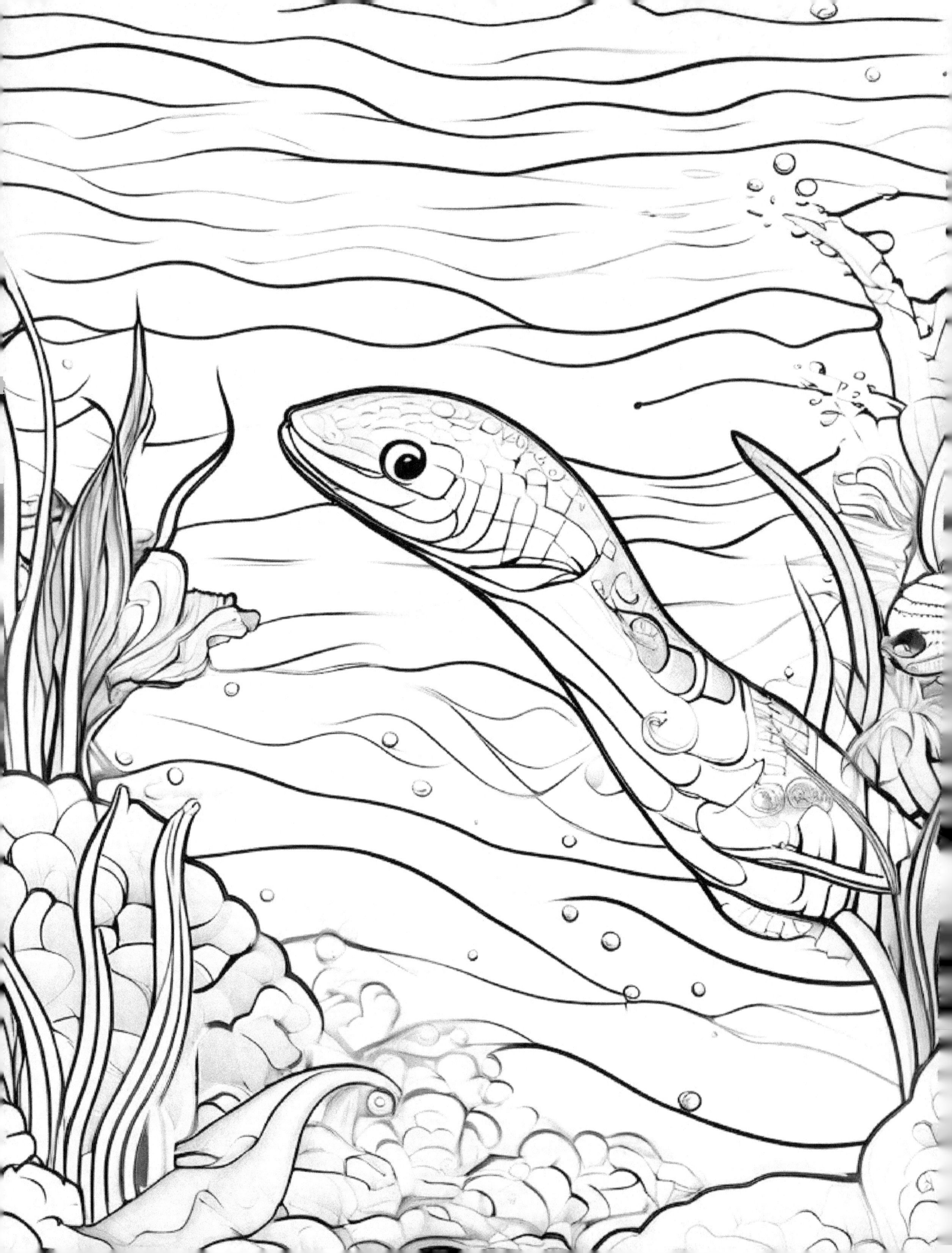

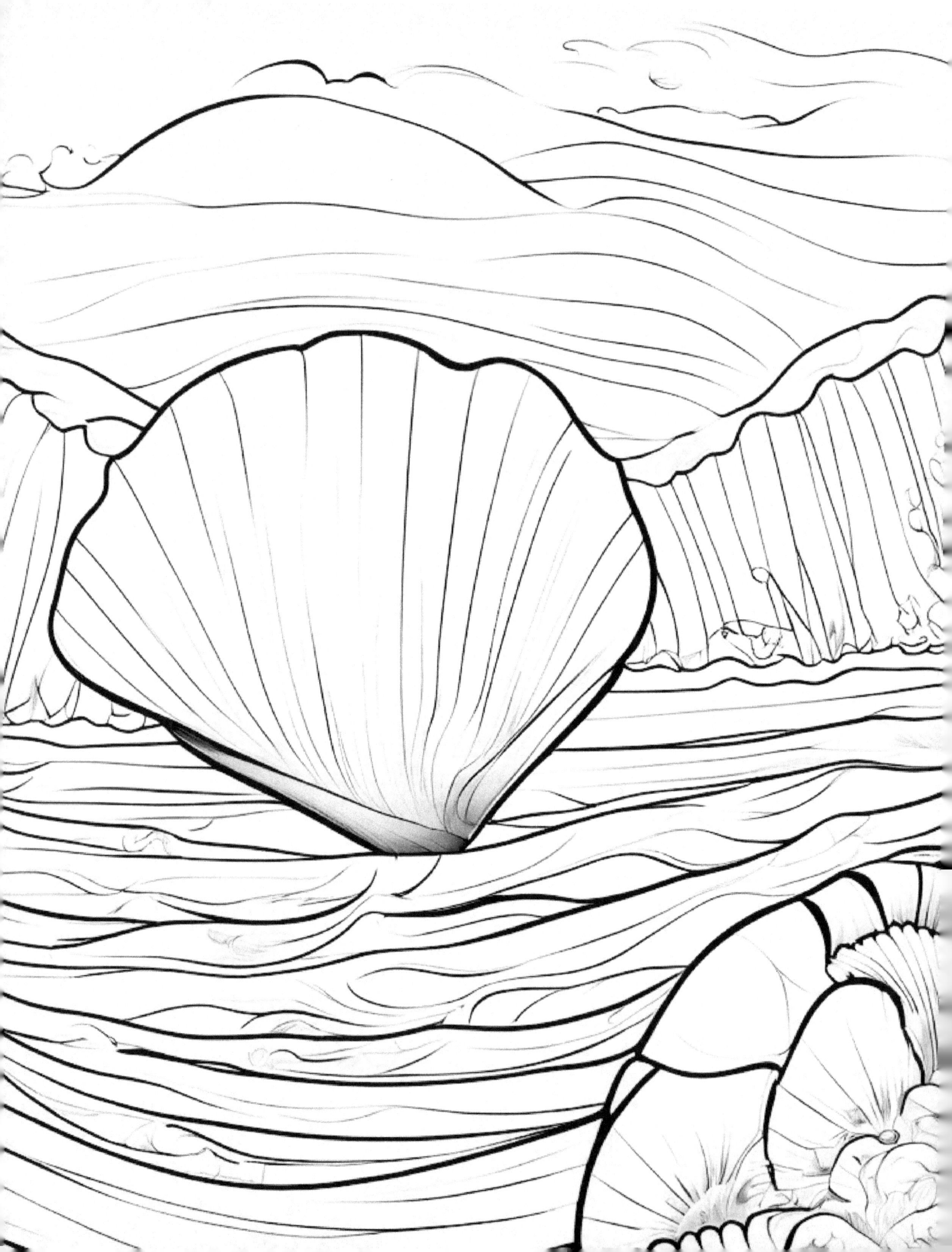

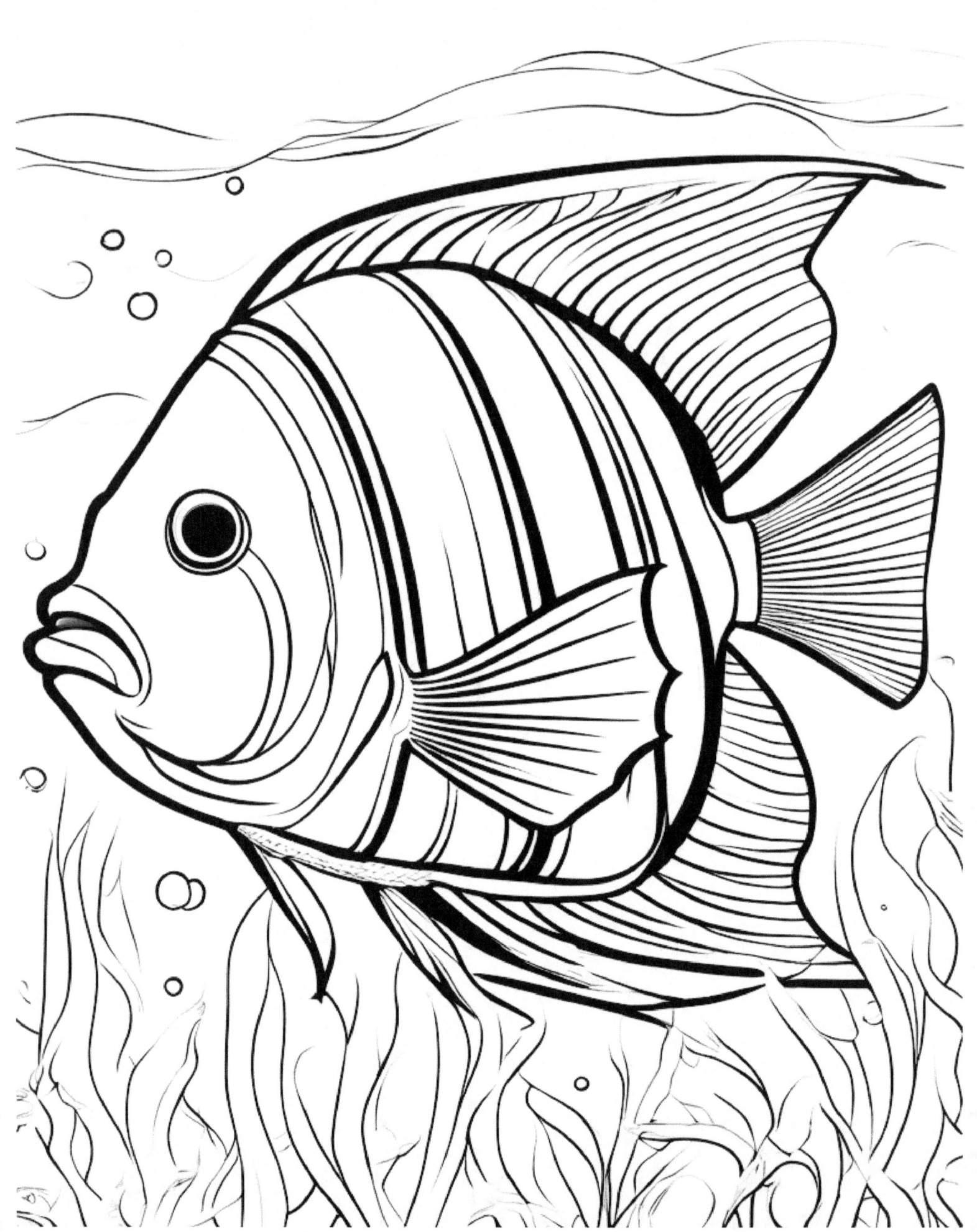